Tourism Policy and Strategy

We work with leading authors to develop the strongest educational materials bringing cutting-edge thinking and best learning practice to a global market.

Under a range of well-known imprints, including Financial Times/Prentice Hall, Addison Wesley and Longman, we craft high quality print and electronic publications which help readers to understand and apply their content, whether studying or at work.

Pearson Custom Publishing enables our customers to access a wide and expanding range of market-leading content from world-renowned authors and develop their own tailor-made book. You choose the content that meets your needs and Pearson Custom Publishing produces a high-quality printed book.

To find out more about custom publishing, visit
www.pearsoncustom.co.uk

A Pearson Custom Publication

Tourism Policy and Strategy

By Paul Fidgeon

PEARSON

Custom
Publishing

Pearson Education Limited
Edinburgh Gate
Harlow
Essex CM20 2JE

And associated companies throughout the world

Visit us on the World Wide Web at:
www.pearsoned.co.uk

First published 2008

ISBN 978 1 84776 158 3

Printed and bound in Great Britain by Henry Ling Limited at the Dorset Press,
Dorchester DT1 1HD

Contents

BACKGROUND AND CONTENT

The structure of this text has been designed to allow for the systematic study of tourism policy and strategy. From initial discussion of how the policy is formulated, later chapters will examine the application of policy guidelines both within a geographical and organisational framework.

Each chapter places a strong emphasis on creative thinking, problem solving and directed independent study. Having studied the text the reader should understand:

- The nature of tourism policy

- How tourism policy is derived.

- The philosophical underpinning on which tourism policy is developed.

- The motivation(s) for translating a general philosophy of tourism into a series of specific operational policy objectives within a country or organisation.

- The opportunities for, and constraints imposed upon, the process of policy formulation.

- Key development strategies for the attainment of policy objectives.

- How and what organisational structures are established to implement development strategies.

- Various models of policy formulation and the success, or otherwise, of a number of policy initiatives.

Throughout, the aim of the text is to widen the readers' knowledge of policy and its relevance to the tourism industry. The orientation is essentially global drawing, in particular, on developments in Europe and North America. The text also takes a multidisciplinary perspective coming at the subject from socio-economic, finance, human resource and marketing perspectives.

LAYOUT

This text is divided into 14 chapters. Each chapter includes a range of pedagogical elements each designed to enhance skill acquisition and the development of knowledge. These include:

- Aims

- Objectives

  What you should be able to <u>do</u> having completed the unit.

- Background Discussion

  The theoretical context.

- Study Activities

  Simple tasks designed to meet the aims and objectives of each individual unit.

- Discussion Questions

- Recommended Reading

- Application

  Designed to focus on themes, issues and concepts presented in the forgoing text.

HOW TO USE THIS TEXT

It is not intended that this publication is just a reference book - it is a study guide designed to get the reader thinking about tourism policy and policy-making. The activities contained throughout aim to keep the reader focused on the subject. To this end, any person should be prepared to write down ideas, run around, collect data and discuss information with peers and policy-makers.

Clearly it is impossible for any text to tell the reader everything they need to know about tourism policy. This is where background research comes in. Lookout for suggestions for further reading. These are included at the end of each chapter.

ACKNOWLEDGEMENTS

The author would like to thank the following people without whom the publication of this text would not be possible.

Professor Brent Ritchie, University of Calgary, Alberta, Canada

Don Anderson, CEO, Calgary Visitor and Convention Bureau

Professor Michael Hall, Head of Tourism, University of Wellington, New Zealand

Professor Steven Page, Highlands & Islands Chair of Tourism, University of Stirling

Peter Williams, Whistler Chair of Tourism, Simon Fraser University, British Columbia, Canada

Pacific Rim Institute of Travel & Tourism

Khalda, Julie, Kay, Jenny and the girls in the Secretarial Services Unit at TVU.

Paul Fidgeon
Principal Lecturer in Tourism
Thames Valley University

Introduction to Policy

CHAPTER 1

Introduction to Tourism Policy

CHAPTER OUTLINE

Studying tourism policy.

What is policy?

Understanding tourism policy.

Approaches to the study of tourism policy.

Summary.

CHAPTER OBJECTIVES

Having read this chapter and undertaken the necessary study activities you should understand:

- The various conceptual and philosophical approaches to the study of tourism policy.

- What is meant by the terms policy and tourism policy.

- Why it is necessary to study tourism policy.

- The regulations, rules, guidelines, directives and strategies that constitute a typical tourism policy.

- Who is responsible for formulating tourism policy.

- What opportunities and constraints influence tourism policy and tourism policy-makers.

- How it is possible to analyse tourism policy within geo-political and various organisational frameworks.

STUDYING TOURISM POLICY

Hall and Jenkins (2006) remind us that tourism is the world's largest industry and is expected to continue to grow. In addition to being a major economic, environmental and socio-cultural force it is also a highly political phenomenon. The nature of tourism in any given community is the product of complex inter-related economic and political factors, as well as particular, geographic and recreational features that attract "outsiders".

While the economics of tourism and tourism geography have received considerable attention, studies of the politics of tourism and in particular tourism policy and the policy making process are scant. (Hall 2004)

Nevertheless policy is a focal point of government activity. Tourism has also become an integral part of government machinery in both developed and lesser developed countries. In the UK the latter is illustrated through the establishment and workings of the Visit Britiain and the National Tourist Boards. Despite this emphasis on policy and specialisation in government, critics have voiced concern about the 'excesses' and 'mistakes' of national tourism development policies as well as the dearth of general policy initiatives.

Academic studies of tourism policy have traditionally adopted one of three approaches:

1.   The study of the causes and consequences of policy decisions vis:

- What socio-economic, political and/or environmental characteristics share the content of policy?

- What impact does tourism policy have on society?

2.   An analysis of the causes and consequences of tourism policy from a particular disciplinary perspective.

      A sociological methodology and philosophy for example might be brought to bear in understanding policy problems and processes.

3.   The evaluation of the success (or otherwise) of policy initiatives against set criteria - whatever these might be.

Study Activity 1

See if you can track down an example of any one of the aforementioned approaches.

e.g.   Holden A (2005) Tourism Studies and the Social Sciences, Routledge.

The focus of studies in tourism policy have, like the conceptual and philosophical framework of the subject, concentrated on specific topics. Namely:

1.   The political nature of the tourism policy making process.

2.   Public participation in policy making.

3.   Sources of power in tourism policy making.

4.   The analysis of complex policy environments.

5.   Perceptions as to the effectiveness of tourism policies.

Hall (2004) has suggested that progress in these areas has, to date, been hindered by the limited amount of qualitative and quantitative studies in tourism policy; the lack of well defined analytical and theoretical frameworks for policy analysis; and a lack of comparative data and case studies pertaining to the policy making process. Given these structural weaknesses it is not surprising that governments and organisations have struggled to comprehend the tourism industry and how they should intervene.

It might be possible to hypothesise that there is an element of inexperience in tourism policy formulation and implementation particularly as much government activity in the tourist industry is relatively recent as compared with other traditional concerns of government such as education, employment or social welfare. In the public sector policies remain weak, incremental and ad hoc. This is despite the fact perceptions of the tourist industry have advanced rapidly.

Study Activity 2

Outline any tourism policy initiatives you are aware of. Who was responsible for initiating or implementing such initiatives?

WHAT IS POLICY?

Inevitably the question must be raised what is meant by the term policy?

Policy making is first and foremost a political activity. It is influenced by the economic, social and cultural characteristics of society. In the public sector it is also influenced by the formal structures of government and other features of the political system. Values, ideologies, power and institutional frameworks all come together to influence decision-making processes.

Given the interaction of numerous forces in the policy making process (e.g. individuals, agencies, laws, perceptions, ideas, choices, processes and power) it is not surprising to find that there is little agreement in policy studies as to what policy is, how to identify it and how to clarify it. As Cunningham (1963) suggests "Policy is like an elephant - you recognise it when you see it but cannot easily define it."

Several definitions of policy have been put forward. (Jenkins 1978), (Anderson 1984), (Dye 1992).

1. Policy is: "A set of related decisions taken by a political actor or group of actors concerning the selection of goals and the means of achieving them within a specified situation where these decisions should, in principle, be within the power of these actors to achieve". (Roberts 1971: 152-153, in Jenkins 1978: 15)

2. Policy is: "The relationship of a government unit or organisation to its environment". (Andersen 1984: 3)

3. Policy is: "All the courses of action carried out by authorities. Authorities are those who have a means of physical force at their disposal, e.g. parliamentary, executive and judicial officers. Policy is what is done in their official capacity ... and by all other members of offices, bureaux, directorates, services or organisations ... who work under them". (Forward 1974: 1)

4. Policy is: "Whatever governments/organisations choose to do or not to do". (Dye 1992)

5. Policy is: "A course of action or inaction chosen by authorities to address a given problem or inter-related set of problems". (Pal 1992: 2)

In all these definitions policy implies a deliberate choice between alternatives. It also requires that it is processed, authorised or ratified by agencies that may or may not lie within the framework of government. Pressure groups, community leaders, street level bureaucrats and others all work inside and outside the policy arena established by the state, a company or organisation and influence and perceive policies in different ways.

UNDERSTANDING TOURISM POLICY

Hall and Jenkins (2006) define tourism policy as

"Whatever governments, companies or organisations choose to do or not to do with respect to tourism."

Ritchie (1997) takes a more prescriptive approach.

Tourism policy is:

"A collection of regulations, rules, guidelines, directives and development/ promotion objectives and strategies which provides a framework within which collective and individual decisions affecting tourism development and daily activities within the industry are taken."

Study Activity 3

Why do you think it is important to study tourism policy?

Study Activity 4

What types of regulations, rules, guidelines, directives, objectives and strategies do you think the tourism industry should be concerned about?

In relation to study activity 3, tourism policy is important:

- Because it defines the rules of the game - the terms under which tourism operators must function.

- It sets out activities and behaviours that are unacceptable.

- It provides a common direction and guidance for all tourism stakeholders (or interest groups) within a destination.

- It facilitates consensus around specific strategies and objectives for a given destination.

- It provides a framework for public/private discussions on the role and contributions of the tourism sector to the economy and to society in general.

- It allows tourism to more effectively interface with other sectors of the economy.

Because of the foregoing, it is important to keep in mind that tourism policy affects the extent to which all day to day operational activities - such as marketing, event development, attraction operation, and visitor reception programs - are successful. As such, it is not just a theoretical concept - it has very real implications in everyday practice.

According to the UK Department of National Heritage tourism policy at the national level deals with:

- Taxation - types and levels

- Financing for the tourism sector

- The nature and direction of product development & maintenance

- Transportation access & infrastructure

- Regulatory practices (e.g. airlines, travel agencies)

- Environmental practices & restrictions

- Industry image, credibility

- Community relationships

- Human resources & labour supply

- Union & labour legislation

- Technology

- Marketing practices, and

- Facilitating foreign travel (both inbound and outbound)

Clearly tourism policy is affected by other rules, regulations and directives many of which come from other fields with which tourism must interface. In the UK these include the Department of Trade and Industry and the European Union (to mention just two). Although these are often beyond the control of tourism policy formulators and decision-makers these must also be understood if sense is to be made of the implications of range of policy directives on the tourism industry.

Study Activity 5

What kinds of policies (rules, regulations, standards, directives and strategies) controlled by governments and other industry sectors and organisations are likely to have an effect on the tourism industry and how?

In answering study activity 5, hopefully you were able to identify some of the following criteria:

- Taxation - affects costs and thus profitability

- Interest rate policy - affects costs and thus profitability

- Bilateral air agreements - determines foreign visitor access

- Environmental policy - limits growth and access to attractive, but sensitive areas.

- Customs and immigration policy - can facilitate or hinder international visitation

- Communications policy - can restrict use of certain advertising media

- Minimum wage policy - can affect labour markets (where appropriate)

- Welfare policy - can influence nature and behaviour of workforce

- Education policy - can affect quality of workforce

- Cultural policy - can affect preservation and promotion of national heritage

- Foreign investment policy/regulations - can affect availability of investment capital

- Local zoning policy/by-laws - can restrict or encourage tourism facility development

- National/Provincial/Local policy re: funding support for major public facilities (e.g. stadiums, convention centres, museums, parks) - can drastically affect destination attractiveness

- Infrastructure policy - can directly determine the quality of roads, bridges, water quality and cleanliness

- Health care policy - can make destination safer for visitors, or restrict resident travel to foreign destinations

7

- Currency/Exchange rate policies - directly affects destination costs and competitiveness

- Legal system - determines consumer/visitor protection legislation (e.g. liability for failing to deliver advertised facilities/tours/experiences

To summarise - there are a whole range of social, economic, legal and technological policies that greatly affect the appeal, attractiveness and competitiveness of a tourism destination. Some are under the control of the tourism sector (such as visitor satisfaction guarantee policy, truth in advertising policy) but the great majority are not. Thus, the challenge facing tourism managers is to try and influence global policies where they can - and adapt to them as effectively as possible where they cannot.

Given the nature of tourism it may be appropriate to reflect on who has responsibility for developing rules, regulations and directives (i.e. policy) for the tourism industry at a given destination.

At the local/city level it is common to find policy emanating from the following organisations: Convention and Visitor Bureau/local Tourist Boards, Economic Development Authorities or the local Chamber of Commerce.

At the regional level, regional tourist boards e.g. The Southern Tourist Board, Cumbria Tourist Board (UK) and marketing consortia e.g. Alberta Tourism Partnership (Canada) play important roles.

At the county or urban borough level departments of tourism e.g. Humberside Tourism, Department of Tourism and Leisure Services - Borough of Waltham Forest, can be found. Frequently the tourism policy function is combined with other areas of economic activity, culture, parks and recreation and/or entrepreneurial services. Partnership organisations (see Tourism Industry Issues) and Tourism Development Agencies may also have a role in policy formulation at this level. The reader's attention is drawn to the work of London 2012 and efforts to modernise the London Tube

Finally at the National level outside Canada and the United States tourism policy making rests largely with the national tourist boards. In Great Britain the 1969 Development of Tourism Act empowered the three main National Tourist Boards with a tourism policy making function.

Study Activity 6

Review a range of policy directives initiated by your national tourist board. What do they propose?

It should be noted that at the **international** level, there are two major organisations having a major interest in providing direction to the tourism sector. The **World Tourism Organisation (WTO)**, an affiliate of the United Nations, is made up of member states. Thus, it has a governmental orientation. The areas of policy interest of the WTO related to international travel have been research/statistics, security of travel (anti-terrorism, health), facilitation of travel (visa policy), education policy for tourism, and more recently, environmental protection.

The **World Travel and Tourism Council (WTTC)** is a private sector organisation whose membership consists of some 60 of the largest corporations involved in tourism (airline firms are especially active). The WTTC was originally conceived of, and established by American Express. Areas of policy focus of the WTTC have been taxation and the environment.

Given the different levels of tourism policy it may be appropriate to ask who should be in charge of making tourism policy?

In countries as large, geographically diverse and politically complex as France and Spain efforts to formulate tourism policy at the national level have met with little success. This is not the case in smaller, more unified countries such as Switzerland and Singapore.

In Great Britain the tendency has been for provincial governments (or counties) and the regional tourist boards to become major players with respect to tourism policy - primarily through the structure plan process and regional tourism plans.

Many researchers (Ritchie 1997, Getz 1997) have questioned whether the city state model of tourism leadership may be the most effective. For those cities that clearly have an attractive and viable tourism "product", it would seem that their closeness to the market, their close working relationship with the industry, their ability to provide more evident direct benefits, and their consequent ability to generate citizen support for tourism development, has given them a growing role in tourism policy. The growing significance and policy impact of such cities - that have collectively formed the **International Association of Convention & Visitor Bureaux (IACVB)** - is increasingly evident. The problem of course is that many tourism areas are not located in city states.

There can, of course, be conflicts among policy makers in the different jurisdictions. When international visitors make a trip to London in their mind are they visiting Great Britain, England, the South-East or the Capital? Seen in this light it raises the question who should be responsible for tourism policy relative to this type of visitor? Some might say it does not matter. The problem is that it does because:

• Who should pay for the promotion of the capital? The city itself (via Visit London)? the region (via the South Eastern Tourist Board?); the country (via the Visit England) or all of the constituent parts of the British Isles (via Visit Britiain).

• Similarly the question can be raised, who should be responsible for the cost of research to study potential London tourist markets?

Other issues centre around:

• How should competing bids from other cities/regions for major international events be organised and allocated? Prior to its successful bid, London found itself locked in a battle with the City of Manchester to attract the 2,000 Summer Olympic games.

• How should the city be represented within various tourism policy making organisations? Again through local regional and national tourist offices?

• How should funds for general and tourism infrastructure be allocated? For example, to the capital or the region(s)?

• How should taxation receipts be distributed?

AN OVERVIEW OF APPROACHES TO THE STUDY OF TOURISM POLICY

The study of policy is a separate academic discipline in its own right. It is an area of academic scholarship that generates much debate, research and literature. Interest in policy research started in Britain in the 1960s as social scientists became attracted by the applied, multi-disciplinary, problem directed nature of policy analysis.

There remains no dominant or coherent approach to policy studies (Brooks 2003). Policy research has been built up on two main types of theory - those that adopt prescriptive models and those which adopt descriptive models.

Prescriptive models seek to demonstrate how policy making should occur relative to pre-established standards or criteria. Descriptive models document the way in which the policy process actually occurs. Prescriptive models serve as a guide to an ideal situation. However, a descriptive approach is preferred when exploring a new territory in a particular policy arena. Descriptive models also give rise to explanations about what happened during the decision-making and policy making processes. They help analysts to understand the effects that choice, power, perceptions, values and processes have on policy making.

Be warned that the dynamics of the policy making process in the tourism industry can be incredibly complex. Understanding how a policy is formulated and implemented can be difficult. Things are made worse by the fact that policy formulation and implementation can be difficult to separate on a consistent basis because policy is often formulated as it is implemented and vice versa.

Further complexity can be introduced in that studies can analyse different stages in the policy process and different levels of analysis (i.e. from the micro level of decision-making within an organisation through to an analysis of policy formulation and the impact of a policy on the wider tourism industry).

SUMMARY

This chapter has attempted to combine the theoretical study of tourism policy vis-definitions, concepts, models and approaches - with a more practical analysis of what tourism policy actually means in terms of establishing regulations, rules and guidelines and who is responsible for establishing policy in the tourism industry. It has been shown that policy can be analysed at several levels. Similarly the outcomes and impacts of tourism policy can be studied within the organisational framework of several jurisdictions.

The past decade has seen tourism policy receiving growing interest and recognition as a legitimate area of study; hence the evaluation of organisational decisions, actions and programmes. It has been shown that complex policies have initiated extensive investigations into processes, outcomes and adjustments. Tourism policy studies have sought to reflect on who gets what, when and why in the policy process and make a contribution to better informed decision and policy making.

DISCUSSION QUESTIONS

1. Why should academics be interested in tourism policy?

2. Why has it proved so difficult to study the process of tourism policy formulation and implementation?

3. Outline the different approaches that academic studies have traditionally adopted towards studying tourism policy.

4. How might it be possible to analyse different levels of tourism policy within a company or organisation?

5. What do you take to understand by the terms policy and tourism policy?

6. What factors influence the process of tourism policy formulation?

7. What destination management organisations traditionally have responsibility for developing tourism policies?

8. How might there be conflicts among policy makers in different geo-political jurisdictions?

9. Outline the different types of regulations, rules, guidelines and directives typically found in a tourism policy.

APPLICATION

Does your country have a national tourism policy? If so identify and critically evaluate the policy's stated goals and objectives. If not, discuss the reasons as to why such a policy does not exist, or is only in its formative stages.

RECOMMENDED READING

Anderson, J E, (1984) Public Policy Making, CBS College Publishing, New York

Dye, T, (1992) Understanding Public Policy, Prentice Hall, 7th Edition

Hall, C M, Jenkins, J, (2006) Tourism and Public Policy, 3rd Edition, Routledge

Hall, C M, (1994) Tourism and Politics : Policy, Power and Place, Belhaven Press, London

Hogwood, B, Gunn, L, (1984) Policy Analysis for the Real World, Oxford University Press

Richter, L K, (1989) The Politics of Tourism in Asia, University of Hawaii Press

Ritchie, J R, Goeldner, C R, (1997) Travel, Tourism and Hospitality Research, Wiley and Sons Ltd

Tribe J (2005) Corporate Strategy in Tourism, 2nd Edition, Routledge

CHAPTER 2

Policy and Politics

INTRODUCTION

Despite tourism being widely regarded as the world's largest industry and its consequent effects on national and regional economies; the political aspects of tourism are rarely discussed in the tourism literature. Over twenty five years ago Matthews wrote, 'the literature of tourism is grossly lacking of political research' (1975, p 195). Today, the same comment still holds true. Despite the vast amount of research currently being conducted elsewhere in the social sciences on tourism-related subjects, the politics of tourism is still the poor cousin of both tourism research and political science and policy studies.

TOURISM AND POLITICS

The relationship between politics and tourism is *not* primarily concerned with political parties and elections and their influence on tourism policy, although this is, of course, an aspect of the politics of tourism, The study of politics is inexorably the study of power. '*Politics is about power, who gets what, where, how and why*' (Lasswell, 1936). There are five major elements to politics. First, it is concerned with the activity of making decisions in and for a collection of people, whether it be a small group, a community, an organisation or a nation. Secondly, it is about decisions and the various policies and ideologies which help establish the various choices which affect decisions. Thirdly, it is concerned with the question of who makes the decisions, one person or an élite, and how representative they are. Fourthly, politics is interested in the processes by which decisions are made and the various institutions within which they are made. Finally, politics is concerned with how decisions are implemented and applied to the community.

Study Activity 1

Think about a piece of tourism policy. LHR T5 is a particularly good one here.

1.   *Who was involved in making those rules, regulations, guidelines or directives? (i.e. policy)*

2.   *How was that policy influenced by a prevailing (political) ideology?*

3.   *Go back to question 1. Who within that group had the most power to influence policy decisions?*

4.   *How were decisions made?*

5.   *How will the policy be implemented?*

The mainstream of tourism research has either ignored or neglected the political dimension of the allocation of tourism resources, the generation of tourism policy, and the politics of tourism development. Not that political science has contributed much to the study of tourism.

Apart from the notable efforts of Matthews (1983) and Richter (1989), political science has all but ignored the role of tourism in modern society. Defence, housing, health, energy, environmental issues and social policy have all been studied in depth by political scientists and policy analysts throughout the world, but tourism has rarely been touched upon.

And yet tourism can be used for political means. It can be used as a means of economic development, it can be used as a way of redistributing wealth, it can even be used to showcase the political achievements of a particular government.

Study Activity 2

Give some examples of how tourism can be used for political means.

Tourism policy, the nature of government involvement in tourism, the structure of tourist organisations and the nature of tourism development all emerge from a political process. To understand tourism and its related impacts, we must therefore understand its inherently political nature.

POLITICAL STUDIES IN TOURISM

As we have noted, research into the political dimensions of tourism has received relatively little attention both in the field of tourism and in the area of policy analysis. Perhaps there are several reasons to account for this.

- There is an unwillingness on the part of many decision makers both in government and in the private sector to acknowledge the political nature of tourism

- There is a lack of official interest in conducting research into the politics of tourism

- Tourism is not regarded as a serious scholarly subject

- There are substantial methodological problems in conducting political and administrative studies in tourism.

Study Activity 3

What evidence is there to support these statements?

All of this stands in marked contrast to focus on the 'practical' or 'applied' aspects of tourism studies. Think of your own degree. While much attention has been applied to the economic dimensions of tourism or aspects of marketing, HRM or finance, very little attention has been paid to the wider philosophical, societal or political dimensions of the subject. Your degree reflects what is going on in education and in society as a whole ie that detailed policy studies are few and far between and the few that there are have tended to focus on issues pertaining to investment, employment and the economic benefits of tourism rather than ideals of power, power-relations, equality and social justice.

THE POLITICAL DIMENSIONS OF TOURISM

The underlying assumption of this text is that politics and tourism policy are inexorably linked. Hall (1994) gives some examples of how.

i.   Politics can determine tourism flows vis: who can travel, where, and what they can see (visitor management).

ii.   It determines how a region is promoted – to who and by whom.

iii.   Politics determines what is built, where and by who.

iv.   Politics determines levels of tourism expenditure.

v.   Taxation e.g. departure and environmental taxes.

vi.   Customs and excise regulations.

vii.   Visa requirements.

viii.   Access to tourist destinations.

ix.   Tourist carrying capacity – and limits of tourist expansion.

x.   The long term viability of tourist destinations eg the decision to extend the resort life-cycle.

xi.   Financial aid to tourist projects.

xii.   The possibility for profits to be repatriated.

xiii.   The employment of local labour.

xiv.   Tourist health, safety and security.

xv.   The tourism planning process.

xvi.   How tourism projects will be evaluated.

xvii.   Politics determines consumer rights and interests.

xix.   It determines how the tourism industry should be organised and regulated.

xx.   Politics affects ideology (our system of beliefs).

Study Activity 4

Try and give some examples of policies that have facilitated the above.

WHO BENEFITS FROM TOURISM POLICY?

A simplistic answer would be governments, the tourism industry or the consumer. A more reflective answer is that politics is about control. This being the case bodies or organisations with the greatest degree of political control are in the most advantageous position to influence the policy agenda. (i.e. policy aims and objectives) and benefit from them.

Study Activity 5

In the LHR T5 planning enquiry do you believe that all the 'actors' involved in the decision to build a fifth terminal had an equal voice? If not, why not?

The evidence equally suggests the benefits and costs of tourism policy are not always evenly spread throughout a host community.

Study Activity 6

Again in the case of LHR T5 how so?

As Greenwood (1976, p141) observed in his study of the impacts of tourism on the Spanish Basque municipality of Fuenterrabia, 'only the local people have learned about the "costs" of tourism. The outside investors and the government have been reaping huge profits and are well satisfied.' Greenwood's study is interesting because it illustrates that inevitably in the development of any policy there must always be an element of political conflict. Groups of human beings are in constant struggle with each other over the potential impact of a political decision or the allocation of resources. In the case of our LHR example, BAA's loss is the environmentalists gain or LHR's loss is Stanstead's gain.

In the policy making process power is crucial. Understanding how much political power each group has (power-relationships) can help us understand why a particular set of rules, regulations or directives were made. There are always in policy making winners and losers. Only now is attention starting to be turned as to whether the 'cards' are being stacked against certain groups/individuals or organisations in the tourism political arena.

Study Activity 7

Think of some examples, not necessarily from tourism, of where politics and political bias has possibly excluded certain groups from the policy decision-making process. How were these groups excluded or disadvantaged when it came to defending or promoting their vested interests?

STUDYING THE POLITICAL DECISION-MAKING PROCESS

How is policy formulated? Later Chapters in this text will review the work of Fidgeon and Ritchie (1997) and Mintzberg (1997). However, Hall (1994) notes that the policy making process is complicated. The reasons for this have much to do with politics.

• Political values and ideologies (our fundamental beliefs) change.

- At any one moment in time there are always conflicting political beliefs.

- There is no one (or ideal) theoretical model on which to base the formulation of tourism policy. Not everyone believes that Fidgeon is right!!

- It is often unclear who should formulate tourism policy – academics, professional bodies, individual companies, the general public? Indeed all of them or some of them? If so, who? And how many from each group?

CONCLUSION

This chapter has attempted to highlight the relationship between politics, tourism and policy. The unit has highlighted the dearth of literature in this field.

It has been shown that politics is about power and control. Power-relationships have been analysed and discussed in terms of how they influence policy-making.

DISCUSSION QUESTIONS

1. What is meant by the terms political power and control?

2. How are these concepts unequally distributed in society?

3. Give an example of where political power and control has come to influence a policy decision

4. Reflect on who are the 'political losers' in society. What evidence is there to suggest that some individuals or organisations are always destined to be losers?

5. How might your chance of being a political 'winner' or 'loser' be determined by your ideology?

RECOMMENDED READING

Hall, C M, (1994) *Politics, Power and Place*, Chapter 1, Belhaven Press, London

Richter, L K, (1989) *The Politics of Tourism*, University of Hawaii Press

Sur, B, (1999) *Winners and Losers : Politics and Tourist Development*, Policy Studies Review 10 2/3: 130-137

Wong, G M, (1996) *Politics: Who gets what, when and how*, McGraw-Hill.

CHAPTER 3

Tourism Policy For The Competitive Destination & Organisation

CHAPTER OUTLINE

Introduction

The Concept of Competitiveness

The World Economic Forum Model of Global Competitiveness

Developing a Model of Competitiveness for Tourism

International Competitiveness in a Tourism Context

Dimensions of Competitiveness

Dimensions of Attractiveness

Deterrents to Visitation

Marketing and Managerial Efforts to Enhance Appeal

Internal Organisation and External Alliances

Effectiveness and Efficiency of Delivery

Defining and Measuring Tourism Related Prosperity

Establishing Competitive Strength and Positioning

Developing a Competitiveness Model

The Operationalisation of the Model

Summary

CHAPTER OBJECTIVES

Having read this chapter and undertaken the necessary study activities you should understand:

- The factors that determine the competitiveness of a tourism destination.

- How policy might be formulated and designed to enhance destination competitiveness.

INTRODUCTION

Study Activity 1

One of the primary goals of tourism policy is to provide frameworks and decision guidelines that will serve to increase the attractiveness and competitiveness of any tourism company destination or organisation.

> - *How would you define destination attractiveness?*
> - *How would you define company organisational competitiveness?*
>
> *In your efforts to define these terms, attempt to highlight the differences between the two concepts.*

List the factors which you believe determine destination attractiveness and organisational competitiveness

Note the major differences between the two concepts.

During the past decade, many of the world's traditional destinations and most respected tourism companies have awakened to the reality that their share of the tourism market is declining. In certain cases, this reality was cushioned by the fact that tourism is still growing strongly, albeit slower than the international average. This has been the situation, for example, in Europe and Canada. In other cases, for example, companies such as My Travel have witnessed an actual decline in their number of clients and tourism receipts.

THE CONCEPT OF COMPETITIVENESS

Growth and decline is a product of individual companies and countries being integrated into the global economy and being driven by market forces. Two major analytical frameworks have been developed to understand global competitiveness. While neither focus directly on tourism they provide a useful starting point for the development of a more sector specific approach.

i) **The Porter Model of Competitive Advantage**

With respect to individual firms, Porter's thesis is that they must possess some particular competitive advantage if they are to achieve competitive success. This competitive advantage may take the form of either low cost or differentiated products that command premium prices. In order to be successful, a firm must develop a competitive strategy which enables it to perform more effectively than its competitors, either through the ability to produce and market a given product more efficiently, or to provide a distinctive product which can be sold at a premium price. To create a competitive advantage, it is necessary for a firm to find better ways to compete and to exploit them globally by continually upgrading the firm's products and processes. The actual choice of a particular strategy reflects the skill of management in responding to "five competitive forces", namely: threat of entry, bargaining power of buyers and suppliers, degree of competitive rivalry, and the threat of substitutes. These five forces together, it is argued, determine industry profitability (Moutinho 2000).

The importance of the nation in determining the competitiveness of a firm relates to the extent to which it either promotes or impedes the firm by shaping the environment in which that firm competes. This environment, according to Porter, is defined by four major attributes:

1. **Factor Conditions:** The nation's position in factors of production such as skilled labour or infrastructure, necessary to compete in a given industry.

2. **Demand Conditions:** The nature of home demand for the industry's product or service.

3. **Related and Supporting Industries:** The presence or absence in the nation of supplier industries and related industries that are internationally competitive.

4. **Firm Strategy, Structure and Rivalry:** The conditions in the nation governing how companies are created, organised, and managed, and the nature of domestic rivalry.

Porter further argues that each of the above determinants does not simply operate independently in defining the national environment but forms part of a mutually dependent system. The determinants, thus individually and as a system, create the context in which a nation's firms compete. A nation will succeed internationally in particular industries where a conducive home environment exists. Such an environment will be dynamic and challenging for domestic firms, it will stimulate them to upgrade and widen their advantages over time. As the requirements for success in particular industries and industry segments differ widely, however, and because any country will only have a limited pool of resources, success is not possible in all industries. Nations although able to enjoy dominance in one industry, might fail miserably in another. Also, nations can perform well in one industry segment but lack competitive advantage in another.

While the Porter model has received widespread recognition, it is by no means accepted as infallible or universally applicable. For example, Rugman (2002) asserts that an analysis of the Canadian economy carried out by Porter is seriously flawed. Furthermore, the Porter model appears to have been largely developed with "sophisticated industries" which export "products". Whether or not the "five forces model" and the "four attributes that shape a competitive environment are applicable to the tourism industry remains to be determined.

ii)   **The World Economic Forum Model of Global Competitiveness**

In this model, country competitiveness is understood as a country's ability to create and sustain economic value relative to its competitors.

The WEF argues that every economy has at its disposal a certain set of inputs (called factors of competitiveness) which can be combined to produce useful output. The WEF model identifies eight major factors (and a total of 330 criteria specific points) which can be pulled together as a weighted sum to define a country's ability to compete in the international marketplace. (Table 3.1)

It is assumed that as the factors of competitiveness are of a higher quality and quantity, the more able a country is at adding economic value and selling its products in domestic and international markets. In other words, the better the pool of factors of competitiveness that a country has available for its entrepreneurs, the more fit the country is in the struggle of survival.

The WEF approach makes an important distinction between the **competitive** and the **comparative** advantage of nations. They argue that under the traditional theory of comparative advantage, countries are better off if they trade the products or services that give them the greatest advantage, or least disadvantage, relative to their possible trading partners. A comparative advantage can be based on having an abundance of natural resources in a country, for example oil, whereas competitive advantage can only be based on an entrepreneur's ability to add value to the available resources, such as by refining the oil.

There are several shortcomings of the model.

1. The model is a static one that assumes the value of a country's natural resources have a constant value over time.

2. The model focuses exclusively on the nation state as the basis for analysis and ignores the emergence of large trading blocs, the decline in importance of national borders, the inter-dependence of economies and the growing significance of the transnational corporation.

3. By aggregating measures of performance the technique may mask fairly wide variations in competitiveness of individual sectors of the economy - including tourism.

Table 3.1   The World Economic Forum Model of Factors of Competitiveness

Factor I   Domestic Economic Strength

Macroeconomic evaluation of the domestic economy overall

Factor II   Internationalisation

The extent to which the country participates in international trade and investment flows

Factor III   Government

The extent to which government policies are conducive of competitiveness

Factor IV   Finance

The performance of capital markets and the quality of financial services

Factor V   Infrastructure

The extent to which resources and systems are adequate to serve the basic needs of business

Factor VI   Management

The extent to which enterprises are managed in an innovative, profitable and responsible manner

Factor VII   Science and Technology

Scientific and technological capacity, together with the success of basic and applied research

Factor VIII People

The availability and qualifications of human resources

4.   The model does not clearly differentiate between the factors which determine competitiveness of a nation and the indicators which are used to measure its competitiveness.

Study Activity 2

The Model of Destination Competitiveness includes reference to GLOBAL FORCES in the macro-environment which can have a major impact on the competitiveness and success of a company or tourism destination.

Outline those factors/forces in the global environment which you believe must be taken into account by those responsible for policy formulation in any tourism company or destination.

From the Global Forces that you have identified, pick the three (3) that you consider to be the most important. For each of these three forces consider;

- *What are the major challenges/difficulties that this force poses to policy makers. What policies/strategies are required to address each challenge?*

- *What are the major opportunities that this force presents to policy makers in a tourism company or destination? What policies/strategies are required to take advantage of such opportunities?*

DEVELOPING A MODEL OF COMPETITIVENESS FOR TOURISM

While it is certainly possible to identify weaknesses in the WEF model of competitiveness, it nevertheless represents perhaps the most useful starting point in any effort to develop a similar or parallel model for the tourism sector. Before doing so, however, it is essential to justify why such a model is needed at all. Indeed, it may be argued, that since tourism is simply one of a number of important sectors in any economy, it is automatically covered by the WEF model. To a certain degree, this assertion is true. An examination of the factors used to define and measure the competitiveness of a country reveals that a large percentage, if not all of them, potentially impact on the ability of a country to compete in the tourism market - just as they strengthen the country's overall ability to compete internationally.

Despite the foregoing reality, there are several arguments for developing a model of competitiveness which focuses specifically on the tourism sector. The most compelling of these arguments relates to the fundamental difference between the nature of the "tourism product" and the more traditional goods and services for which the WEF model was developed. As noted above, the WEF model stresses the difference between comparative and competitive advantage. In particular, this model emphasises that comparative advantage is based on the abundance of natural resources in a country, whereas competitive advantage is based only on a country's ability to add value to the resources. Furthermore, the WEF approach explicitly asserts that "By merely selling its natural richness, a country does not become better off in the long run - a sale must be written of as a minus on the national balance sheet; selling the value added (and not the resources) creates a surplus that a country can then invest in its economic development." For this reason, the WEF model focuses on value-added and ignores comparative advantage.

If we extend the concept of comparative and competitive advantage to international tourism. We arrive at the following: comparative advantage would appear to relate to things like climate, beautiful scenery, attractive beaches, wildlife etc.; on the other hand, competitive advantage would seem to relate to such items as the tourism infrastructure (hotels, events, attractions, transportation networks), the quality of management, the skills of the workforce, government policy etc.

It is when we attempt to directly transfer the WEF approach to tourism that we encounter an important theoretical discrepancy. As noted, the WEF model views the export of resources as taking away from national resources - and thus excludes comparative advantage when assessing a country's ability to compete. In international tourism, however, the strength of these arguments are more tenuous. A country's natural resources are clearly an important source of comparative advantage in international tourism. However, in contrast to the sale of resources such as oil or minerals, tourists do not return home with any significant physical elements from the "exporting" country (other than the odd artefact or photograph). As such, these resources are not depleted, despite the fact that people have paid for their "use". In tourism, the visitors purchase an opportunity to briefly experience such resources as scenery, culture and climate - but this "experience" does not necessarily create a corresponding minus on the national balance sheet. Indeed, the fact that certain visitors have experienced a particular country may enhance its appeal, and therefore increase its value to others.

At the same time, it must be acknowledged that tourism can produce externalities which "must be written off as a reduction in the domestic value-added since it implies that the quality of the national resources has deteriorated. Countries should not be misled into seeking short-term prosperity at long-term cost. Value-added on long-term is what really constitutes the basis for prosperity of nations" (World Competitiveness Report, 1992). Such externalities in tourism include, for example, environmental pollution, the despoliation of scenic areas, social fragmentation, the spread of disease, the encroachment into wildlife habitats and the creation of tourist ghettos.

Despite the possibility of the above externalities, it is argued that the tourism phenomenon represents a fundamentally different form of economic exchange than does the sale of physical resources. Based on this premise, it can be further argued that, in the context of international tourism, both comparative and competitive advantage are important. A possible counter argument is that the natural resources of tourism have no economic value in themselves (although many would argue that value cannot be measured in economic terms alone). That is, for example, a scenic valley has no economic value in itself if only the creatures able to experience the scenery are the local fauna. Building a road into the valley, thus providing access to tourists, does however provide value. As the value is created only by the building of the road, and as the scenery is not "sold" (resulting in a corresponding deletion of natural resources) it can be asserted that the concept of comparative advantage is relevant or operative. In brief, because value has been added, the above example may be said to represent a case of competitive rather than comparative advantage.

Despite this counter argument, there still remains a fundamental difference in the sale of an experience related to a resource as opposed to the sale of the resource itself. Indeed, even physical resources require enhancement (or the adding of value) before they can be sold. Oil or minerals in the ground need to be accessed and physically removed from their original location before they become useful commodities. This process, then is the equivalent of providing access to a beach or a scenic area. From this point onwards, however, the nature of the exchange process is conceptually and fundamentally different.

INTERNATIONAL COMPETITIVENESS IN A TOURISM CONTEXT

While the foregoing discussion provides a useful starting point, it does not resolve the critical issue of how to define competitiveness in international tourism. The reality is that development designed to attract international visitors may have a range of purposes. In the end however, it seems reasonable to focus attention on **economic prosperity**; that is national (or destinations) compete in the international tourism market primarily to foster national (destination) prosperity.

It is recognised that other motives may also underlie efforts to develop international tourism. For example, international tourism provides an opportunity to showcase a country as a place to live, to do business, to invest in, and to trade with. Tourism also facilitates international understanding and promotes peace (D'Amore, 1988). It may even be a tool to further the political goals of a country (Buckley et al, 1989). In the end, however, it is ultimately the long-term economic well-being of the country (destination) which must be the central concern.

Study Activity 4

How might tourism:

i) *Provide an opportunity to showcase a country? (give examples)*

ii) *Facilitate understanding and promote peace? (give examples)*

iii) *Further the political goals of a country? (give examples)*

In developing a model of global tourism competitiveness it is sensible to:

1. Take a long-term view

2. Take into account natural resources

3. Take an aggregate perspective (i.e. review all market segments)

4. Consider outbound tourism as this can represent a considerable drain on a country's balance of payments (i.e. prosperity).

5. Ignore public subsidies given the difficulty in accounting for this reality.

DEFINING AND MEASURING COMPETITIVENESS

Defining and measuring the concept of competitiveness is a complex and demanding task. One of the first and perhaps most important aspects of this task is to clearly distinguish between:

a) Indicators of competitive performance (i.e. historic measures which describe how well a nation or destination has performed in the past with respect to creating or enhancing the prosperity of that nation or destination e.g. growth in GD.

b) Factors which contribute to competitiveness i.e. factors that contribute to or detract from a nation e.g. attitude of the workforce.

Certain variables are difficult to define. For example the levels of expenditure on research or the health of a population - both indicate past prosperity as well as influencing future economic performance.

The WEF overcomes these problems by including both indicators and factors in a National Competitiveness Balance Sheet (Table 3.2).

24

Table 3.2 National Competitiveness Balance Sheet for Germany
(Numbers Indicate Germany's Ranking on Each item)

Overall Ranking: 2

Category	Rank	Subcategory Rank	Subcategory	Item Rank	Item
Domestic Economic Strength	2	2	Performance of the Economy	3	Value Added
				12	Capital formation
				3	Inflation
				11	Private Dual Consumption
				3	Economy forecasts
		3	Performance of Economic Sectors	1	Industrial Production
				3	Capital Goods
				3	Service Sector
				8	Agriculture
Internationalisation	1	1	Foreign Trade	4	Trade Balance
				5	Exports of Goods & Services
				1	Export Diversification
				5	Imports of Goods & Services
				11	Exchange Rates
				21	Tourism
		8	National Protectionism		
		1	Partnerships with Foreign Firms		
		8	Foreign Direct Investment	5	Outward
		3	Cultural Openness	12	Inward
Government	2	2	State involvement in the Economy	1	National dest
				2	Official Reserves
				5	Government Expenditure
				2	State Control of the Industry
		3	Legislative & Regulatory Environment	1	Government Efficiency & Transparency
				8	Improper Practices
				18	Environmental Protection
				14	Agricultural Policies
				14	Managerial Freedom
		11	Monetary & Fiscal Policies	10	
				6	Fiscal Policy
				18	Social Security
		1	Nature of the Competitive Environment		
		6	Socio Political Stability	4	Support for Government Policies
				7	Justice & Security
Finance	5	3	Cost of Capital/State of Return		
		2	Availability of Finance		
		10	Stock Markets		
		4	Financial Services		
		8	Corporate Accounts		

			12	Energy Production
			5	Energy Consumption
	7	Natural Resources	14	Self Sufficiency
			17	Arable Area
Infrastructure 6	3	Business Infrastructure	2	Recycling of
	7	Urban Development		
	3	Entrepreneurship		
			8	Willingness to Delegate
			5	Use of Information Technology
			2	Implementation of Strategies
	6	Management Development	3	Long-term Orientation
			8	International Experience
			5	Employee Relationships
			3	Managerial Constraints
			2	Price/Quality Ratio
	2	Corporate Performance	8	Customer Orientation
			10	Product Development
			1	Social Responsibility
Management 2			1	Products
			6	Productivity
	6	Business Efficiency	18	Labour Costs/Compensation Levels
			9	Remuneration of Top Management
			3	Total R & D Expenditure
	4	R & D Expenditure	3	Business R & D Expenditure
			3	Research Co-operation
			12	Funding of R & D
	3	R & D Personnel	3	Total R & D Personnel
			4	Scientists & Engineers
	3	Intellectual Property Generation	2	Basic Research
			4	Patents
Science & Technology 2			3	R & D in Key Industries
			3	Future R & D Spending
	2	Technology Management	2	Production Technologies
			2	Technology Strategies
			4	Financial Constraints
	2	Population Characteristics		
			6	Education
	3	Educational Structures	8	Literacy
			2	In Company Training
			15	Labour Force
			15	Employment
			2	Unemployment
	11	Employment Structures	9	Working Week
			7	Availability of Skilled People
			13	Equal Opportunity
People 3			4	Industrial Disputes
			3	Worker Motivation
			5	Attitude of the Young People
	4	Attitude of the Workforce	7	Availability of Skilled People
			15	Alcohol l& Drug Abuse
			6	Competitive Values
			8	Cost of Living
	1	Quality of Life	10	Leisure Expenditure
			1	Health

Source: Adapted from WEF (2005)

In looking at the Balance Sheet it is not clear to what extent such measures as "the willingness to delegate", "employee relationships", "management freedom" and "education" are a cause of, or are affected by, competitiveness. At best the WEF choose to overlook these difficulties in order to produce a more understandable report.

DIMENSIONS OF COMPETITIVENESS

The WEF model reports a competitiveness ranking for each country in the tourism sector based on each country's net balance of payments related to international tourism expenditures and receipts. However, for a country's policy makers or managers in the tourism sector who are attempting to improve their competitive position in the international marketplace this is not enough.

Ritchie and Crouch (1992) argue that what is needed is an assessment of:

a)   The characteristics of a region that make it attractive to visit.

b)   The barriers which tend to deter travel to a destination.

c)   The effectiveness of marketing and other managerial efforts to enhance perceived attractiveness.

d)   The effectiveness of internal organisational structures and external strategic alliances in strengthening the destination' ability to influence and attract potential visitors.

e)   The ability of a destination to assemble and interpret information which provides it with insights and understanding that enable it to design and develop high appeal experiences more quickly than competitors and/or at a lower cost.

f)   The capability of a destination (or its constituent parts) to efficiently and effectively deliver a high quality visitor experience.

Only by determining the most important indicators of success concerning the performance of the tourism sector as a contributor to the prosperity of a destination is it possible to establish the relative strength and the positioning of a particular destination in relation to other competitors in the marketplace.

DIMENSIONS OF ATTRACTIVENESS

Study Activity 5

What variables determine the attractiveness of a tourist destination? Could some of these variables equally apply to a company or organisation like Air France or the Association of European Airlines?

Research on the determinants of demand in international tourism has revealed a wide range of important factors.

Mikulicz (2003) has isolated three groups of independent variables which affect demand. These include factors which determine market volume (e.g. population, income, leisure time, education, occupation), factors which influence the cost of travel (e.g. transportation cost, distance and time, and the cost of tourism services including the impact of inflation and exchange rates), and utility image (such as tourist appeal, publicity, information, weather, language, ancestry, etc.).

In a somewhat different vein, Gearing et al. (2006) identified eight major categories of variables (or factors) which determine the attractiveness (an important component of competitiveness) of a tourism destination. These eight factors were identified as Natural Features, Culture and Social Characteristics, General Infrastructure, Basic Services Infrastructure, Tourism Superstructure, Access and Transport Facilities, Attitudes towards Tourists, and Price Levels.

When examining the dimensions of attractiveness from a managerial (rather than a conceptual) perspective it is possible to categorise these dimensions in terms of the ability of the destination to influence their development. For example, tourism policy-makers and managers in a destination can significantly influence the development of tourism facilities (such as hotels) and tourism related events (such as festivals). Similarly they can have some limited influence over the development of social services and infrastructure which tourists utilise.

DETERRENTS TO VISITATION & PARTICIPATION

Not all characteristics of a destination contribute to making it a more attractive or appealing place to visit or company to do business with. In opposition to the positive or motivating factors of the type discussed previously there are also a number of factors which serve to deter, or which act as a barrier to visiting a given destination or doing business with a company or organisation. Some of the more obvious deterrents include stringent entry/trade requirements (such as high cost or difficulty to obtain visas and export permits), political instability, terrorism, and the prevalence of disease. Other dimensions may be either a deterrent or a motivator depending upon the nature of the prospective visitor. Different languages, strange cultures, and specific exchange rates may prove attractive to certain travellers and yet be a major deterrent to business planners. As such any model which attempts to assess the overall appeal of a destination, company or organisation must attempt to measure and explain the relative strength of attractors versus deterrents in both individual and aggregate terms.

MARKETING AND MANAGERIAL EFFORTS TO ENHANCE APPEAL

Enhancing the appeal of a company or destination as a place to visit or organisation to do business with most obviously requires programs which improve upon the various factors of attractiveness and/or which reduce the extent to which the various deterrents make it difficult to visit the destination or do business. Enhancing the appeal of, for example, a destination involves a program of marketing efforts designed to influence the decision process of prospective visitors. These efforts may focus on increasing awareness of the existence of the destination or improving the perceptions of the qualities of the destination which are considered most relevant for different market segments. They may also involve facilitating ease of access to the destination through upgraded distribution channels or through developing a more extensive network of sales contacts. In this regard, it is interesting to note that the WEF, while noting that such factors as Technology and R&D Expenditures enhance (or are assumed to enhance) competitiveness, does not appear to include a Marketing Expenditures measure in their model.

Just as marketing efforts can enhance the appeal of a destination and make it more competitive, so can managerial efforts to reduce the severity of the barriers to trade might be important to commercial business organisations. From this perspective, initiatives such as those that reduce the hassle of trade, improve inter-modal linkages among transportation systems, upgrade security, and to facilitate baggage handling, also contribute to making a company such as an airline more competitive. As for any type of expenditure, however, it is important to ensure that such initiatives are cost effective; that is, they add value which exceeds the cost.

INTERNAL ORGANISATION AND EXTERNAL ALLIANCES

The ability of a destination to effectively organise itself can contribute greatly to its ability to compete more effectively in the tourism marketplace. The tourism sector has traditionally been characterised by such terms as fragmented, unfocused, and uncoordinated. These terms have reflected a historical inability of the many diverse components of the industry to work together in the planning, the development and the marketing of a destination. The recognition of this critical shortcoming has resulted in the emergence of the Destination Management Organisation (DMO). Such an organisation has as its primary function to serve as a coordinating body for the many public and private sector organisations involved in tourism. In more progressive situations, the DMO will also provide the leadership necessary to provide overall direction for tourism development within the destination. While the DMO may have different names in different parts of the world (such as Convention and Visitor Bureau, Syndicat de Tourisme, Officina de Turismo) in all cases their function is to enable the many parts of the tourism sector to work together and thus compete more effectively, than would otherwise be the case.

As the tourism market becomes increasingly global, it has become necessary for both individual firms, as well as destinations, to establish strategic alliances with other organisations and destinations in other industry sectors and in other parts of the world. This phenomenon has been highly visible in the airline sector as many national and international carriers seek to enhance their ability to compete by forming a broad range of working relationships with airlines that compliment their route structures as well as their marketing and technical capabilities. Examples of alliances among National Tourism Organisations are found in Europe where the European Tourism Commission conducts joint research on behalf of its members. More recently Canada and the United States have proceeded along similar lines.

EFFECTIVENESS AND EFFICIENCY OF DELIVERY

In order for a company or destination to achieve prosperity, it is not enough to succeed in attracting visitors or clients. In addition, they must be capable of delivering the experience that has been promised in a cost effective manner. Clearly, it does not make sense to attract visitors and be in a position where the cost of providing the travel experience exceeds the amount which has been paid for the experience. This reality implies that a destination or company must be able to manage both the quality of the service provided and the productivity of the service providers responsible for its delivery.

Given the importance of quality of service (QOS) and productivity, the logical next step in laying the groundwork for model development is to identify those factors which determine or influence these variables. Here again, definitional problems must be addressed. More specifically, what is Quality of Service and how can it be operationally measured? Similarly, what is the nature of Productivity in the context of delivering tourism services and how do we measure both the concept as well as the relative influence of the broad range of factors which affect it? While answers to these questions are not easily forthcoming, such answers must be found as part of the overall process of developing a viable model of competitiveness for the tourism sector.

DEFINING AND MEASURING TOURISM RELATED PROSPERITY

Taken to its logical conclusion, the single most relevant measure of the success of tourism in contributing to the prosperity of a company or nation (destination) is the contribution it makes to increasing either corporate worth (e.g. share values) or the total or the per capita income of residents. However, as in the case of the WEF model, it behoves us to also examine a range of other intermediate performance indicators which are assumed to influence prosperity and which are easier to measure. These indicators include such variables as Visitation Levels/Customer Demand, Tourism/Client Expenditures, Market Share Investment, Employment, Tax Revenues, and Industry Profits.

At this early stage of model development and validation, it would seem prudent to include more rather than fewer prosperity related performance indicators in order to better determine which are most useful from both a theoretical and a practical perspective.

ESTABLISHING COMPETITIVE STRENGTH AND POSITIONING

It is difficult enough to identify and measure the factors which determine competitiveness and prosperity. It is equally, if not more difficult to decide how these measures should be weighted or combined to arrive at a single composite index of competitiveness. This is definitely not a trivial issue. Indeed, perhaps the single most telling criticism of the WEF model is the manner in which it produces the composite rankings of competitiveness. In effect the model seems to brush aside the issue of how each of the factors causally determine competitiveness. It would be possible to address this concern by comparing the competitive rankings with the strength of actual performance over time to see to which extent the two are linked. In the extreme, a PIMS (Buzzell and Gale, 1987) type exercise could be carried out to examine the issues further.

As an alternative to comparing countries along a series of dimensions which are supply or production oriented (that is, they directly evaluate the real or perceived quality of the inputs rather than the quality of the products or services that are the output), it may also be useful to determine a destination competitive image and position in the eyes of the marketplace. Such measures of competitive positioning can be developed from either or both attribute based scales and holistic measures of similarity (Echtner and Ritchie 1992). In any, event, the result is an intermediate, market based assessment of a destination's relationship to its competition.

DEVELOPING A COMPETITIVENESS MODEL

Having set the stage, the critical task is to formulate a model on which to analyse and understand competitiveness.

The most basic hypothesis is that:

1. Destination prosperity = fn(function) competitiveness (in any given sector of the tourism industry.

And

2. Tourism competitiveness   =   fn   Destination appeal
                                            Destination Management
                                            Destination Organisation
                                            Destination Information
                                            Destination Efficiency

When

Appeal = fn destination attractiveness (Table 3.3) and destination deterrents (Table 3.4).

Management = fn marketing efforts (Table 3.5), managerial efforts (Table 3.6).

Organisation = fn destination management organisation capabilities (Table 3.7) and strategic alliances (Table 3.8).

Information = fn management information systems (Table 3.9) and research capabilities (Table 3.10).

Efficiency = fn integrity of experience (Table 3.11) and productivity (Table 3.12).

The model assumes, for example, that tourism competitiveness can be enhanced by a well executed program of destination management; tourism marketing efforts; certain managerial approaches; the ability of the destination to provide a "high integrity" experience, and the efforts and certain key activities of a destination management organisation.

Table 3.3   Determinants of Destination Attractiveness

-    **NATURAL FEATURES**

     * General Topography
     * Scenery
     * Flora and Fauna
     * Proximity to Lakes, Rivers and Oceans
     * Mountains
     * Waterfalls, Hot Springs

-    **CLIMATE**

     * Temperature
     * Amount of Sunshine
     * Winds
     * Amount of Precipitation
     * Humidity/Comfort Index
     * Predictability

- **CULTURE & SOCIAL CHARACTERISTICS**

    * Traditions
    * Gastronomy
    * Language
    * Architecture
    * Religion
    * Handicrafts
    * Education
    * Leisure Activities
    * Work
    * History
    * Dress
    * Art, Sculpture and Music

- **GENERAL INFRASTRUCTURE**

    * Road Network
    * Airports
    * Train System
    * Bus System
    * Fresh Water Supply System
    * Electrical System
    * Sewage System
    * Telecommunications System
    * Medical Services
    * Financial Services
    * Computer Services

- **BASIC SERVICES INFRASTRUCTURE**

    * Retail Shopping Facilities
    * Food Stores
    * Garages/Car Maintenance
    * Gas Stations
    * Drugstores
    * Bookstores/News Kiosks
    * Hairdressers
    * Administrative Offices (Police, Courts, etc.)

- **TOURISM SUPERSTRUCTURE**

    ◆ **Residential Tourism Plant**

        * Hotels
        * Motels
        * Pensions
        * Furnished Apartments
        * Bed and Breakfast
        * Youth/Elder Hostels
        * Camping/Caravanning Facilities
        * Holiday Villages
        * Restaurants

* Fast Food Outlets
* Taverns/Bars

♦ **Receptive Tourism Plant**

For Organisation of Travel

* Tour Wholesalers
* Tour Operators
* Travel Agents
* Car Rental Firms
* Excursions & Sightseeing Agents

For Information and Promotion

* Tourism Information Offices
* Local Convention and Visitor Bureau
* Special Events Organisations

Recreation and Sports Facilities

* Summer Facilities (Golf, Tennis, etc.)
* Winter Facilities (Alpine, X-Country Skiing)
* Water Sport Facilities (Boating, Swimming, Fishing)
* Theatres, Movie Houses
* Casinos
* Night Clubs/Night Life
* Physical Fitness Facilities
* Biking Trails

- **ACCESS AND TRANSPORTATION FACILITIES**

* Physical Distance from Markets
* Time Distance from Markets
* Ease and Quality of Auto Access
* Frequency, Ease and Quality of Air Access
* Frequency, Ease and Quality of Train Access
* Frequency, Ease and Quality of Bus Access

- **ATTITUDES TOWARDS TOURISTS**

* Warmth of Reception by Local Population
* Ease of Communication
* Willingness to Provide Information
* Lack of Hostility Towards Tourism Activities

- **COST/PRICE LEVELS**

* Value for Money of Major Local Services, Food, Lodging and Transportation within the Destination
* Cost of Transportation to and from Destination
* Exchange Rates
* Inflation Rates on Travel Related Services

33

- **ECONOMIC AND SOCIAL TIES**

    * Ongoing Trade Relationships
    * Membership in Professional and Trade Associations
    * Historical or Recent Immigration Flows
    * Common Culture and Language
    * Common Religion

- **UNIQUENESS**

    * Unique Religious Centres
    * Unique Landmarks or Symbols
    * Unique Historical Event Sites
    * Unique Current Event Sites
    * Unique Geography
    * Unique Cultural Remains

Table 3.4   Deterrents to Visitation of a destination

- **SECURITY AND SAFETY**

    * Political Instability/Unrest
    * Probability of Terrorism
    * High Crime Rate
    * Poor Record of Air Control Safety
    * Corruption of Police/Administrative Services

- **HEALTH AND MEDICAL CONCERNS**

    * Poor Quality of Sanitation
    * Prevalence or Outbreak of Disease
    * Poor Quality/Unreliable Medical Services
    * Lack of Availability of Medication
    * Unusual Food and Drink

- **LAWS AND REGULATIONS**

    * Visa Requirements
    * Currency Controls
    * Medical Restrictions
    * Restrictions on Corporate Activities

- **CULTURAL DISTANCE**

    * Inability to communicate
    * Taboos on Behaviour
    * High Levels of Poverty
    * Divergent Value Systems

Table 3.5   Marketing Efforts to Enhance the Appeal of a Tourism Destination

- Creation of a high Level of Destination Awareness

- Development of a Strong Destination Image

- Selection of Appropriate Market Segments.

- Development of Strong Linkages with Tourism Wholesalers and Retailers

- Development of Attractive and Flexible Tour Packages

- Provision of Reliable and Responsive Visitor Services

- Selective Development of Unique Facilities, Events and Programs appropriate to the Destination

- Creation of Landmarks and Symbols which Capture the Spirit of the Destination

Table 3.6   Managerial Initiatives to Strengthen the Competitiveness of a Tourism Destination

- Efforts to Reduce Formal Entry Requirements

- Efforts to Facilitate Arrival at and Departure from the Destination

- Efforts to Ensure the Safety of Visitors

- Efforts to Ensure Fair Treatment of Visitors in all Tourist and Finance Transactions

- Efforts to Provide Accessible and Available Medical Services

- Good Information and Signage

- Foreign Investment Policies

Table 3.7   Key Roles and Activities of the Destination Management Organisation to Enhance Competitiveness

- Serve as a Focal Point for the Coordination of all Industry Activities

- Provide Leadership in the Marketing of the Destination

- Serve as a Catalyst and Facilitator for Tourism Infrastructure and Destination Development

- Provide Common Services which Enhance the Quality of the Visitor's Experience

- Provide Leadership in Expanding the Beneficial Community Impacts of Tourism in the Destination Area

- Liaise with all Levels of Government and Other Public Agencies to Represent the Views of the Industry on Decisions affecting the Tourism Sector

- Provide Specialised Services to Improve the Effectiveness and the Profitability of members of the DMO

- Coordinate the Collection and Dissemination of all relevant Information and Research required by DMO Members and the Sector at Large

- Support the Development and Delivery of Education and Training Programs for DMO Members and the Industry as a Whole

Table 3.8   Examples of Strategic Alliances of Tourism Firms and DMOs to Enhance Competitiveness

- Inter-Airline Marketing and Operations Agreements

- Destination Support from Financial Services Firms in return for Member use and Promotion of the Firm's Services

- Linkages and Joint Marketing Programs between Distant but Similar destinations

- Twinning of Travel Destinations based on Cultural, Historic or Economic Ties

- Joint Research by Similar Destinations in Close Proximity

- DMO-University Linkage Agreements for Long Term Research Collaboration

- Inter-Modal Marketing Agreements

- DMO-Computer Reservation System Agreements

Table 3.9   Principal Components of an Internal Destination Management Information System

- Visitor Statistics which Detail Patterns of Tourist Behaviour

- Performance Measures which Identify Problems

- Economic, Social and Environmental Impacts

- Information which Monitors and Tracks the Attitude of the Local Population Toward the Tourism Industry

Table 3.10   Research Capabilities Which Enable a Destination to Prepare an Effective Strategy

-    Market Segmentation Studies

-    The Ability to Forecast Tourist Demand to Aid Long-Term Planning

-    Tourist Satisfaction Studies which Identify Problems and Opportunities

-    Accountability Research which Assesses the Effectiveness of Destination Promotion

-    The Ability to Monitor and Anticipate Changes in the Tourism Macro-Environment

-    Research which Aids the Development of New Tourist Services

Table 3.11   Initiatives to Enhance the Quality of the Experience Provided by a Tourism Destination

-    Establishment of Standards for Tourism Facilities and Performance of Personnel

-    Programs to Objectively and Subjectively Monitor the Quality of Experience Provided by the Destination

-    Monitoring of Resident Attitudes towards Visitors and Activities and Development of the Tourism Sector

-    Efforts to Ensure Public Awareness of, and Participation in, the Planning Process related to Development of Tourism Facilities, Events and Programs within the Destination

-    Support for both Education and Training Programs for Future and Present Industry Personnel

Table 3.12   Initiatives to Enhance Productivity and Performance Levels within a Tourism Destination

-    Efforts to Establish the Cost of Providing Different Levels of Quality and Various Types of Tourism Experiences

-    Pilot Projects to Assess the Viability and Profitability of New Technology

-    Pilot Projects to Assess the Viability and Profitability of Alternative Facility Designs

-    Training Focused specifically on Improving Performance in Selected Jobs

-    Training Focused on Enhancing Ability of Personnel to Effectively Perform Different Seasonal Tasks

-    Evaluation of the Productivity and Effectiveness of Alternative Organisation Structures for Managing and Delivering Different Tourism Experiences

THE OPERATIONALISATION OF THE MODEL

The next critical step in the process is one of carefully defining exactly how each of the conceptual factors and variables in the model can best be measured in the real world of tourism. This task is not quite as daunting as it might appear at first glance due to the fact that a number of individual pieces of research related to many of the variables have been carried out previously. For example, some previously mentioned work has addressed the measurement issues related to destination image (Echtner and Ritchie, 1992), the determinants of attractiveness of a destination (Ritchie and Zins, 1978), the determinants of international tourism demand (Crouch, 1992), and the quality of service in tourism (Fick and Ritchie, 1991). Similarly, work by Haahti (1986) on competitive positioning of destinations is extremely helpful. In these and other published cases, established definitions and measures are already adopted and require no further elaboration. In other instances, however, further research to develop preliminary measures for subsequent use and testing are required.

The process of building and testing such a model requires a considerable amount of research over an extended period of time. In practical terms, the task of model formulation and validation is an iterative, evolutionary process in which the presently crude framework will be continuously refined and improved. Once a basic model has been developed, it will be necessary to carefully examine the ability of the model to predict the success of destinations at an aggregate level and to relate its many hypotheses to various models of individual choice behaviour which have been proposed (for example, Woodside and Lysonski, 1989).

Additional issues relating to the model also need to be addressed.

Namely:

1.   That it focuses on the right measures of prosperity i.e. does it reflect environmental and social degradation as well as more traditional economic costs.

2.   Can it be applied to different levels of geographical study vis: a town, city, region or country and different companies vis: airlines and tour operators?

3.   A better understanding of the determinants of attractiveness are needed particularly amongst different market segments.

4.   Which components of image truly determine the ultimate decision to (or not to) travel or purchase a good or srvice?

5.   There is a need to further explore the trade-offs between cost and distance that are made by different types of travellers in different choice contexts.

6.   Finally there is the need to provide destination managers with some broad guidelines as to the relative cost-effectiveness of different investments designed to improve the competitiveness of a company organisation or destination.

CONCLUSION

This chapter has sought to identify the factors that determine the competitiveness of a tourism company organisation or destination. It has been argued that increasing competitiveness and achieving prosperity forms the basis of many policy initiatives.

Considerable effort has been directed towards defining and measuring elements of competitiveness. In this context a model of competitiveness has been advocated for tourism policy-makers that sees competitiveness as a function of company/destination attractiveness, management, organisation, information and efficiency.

DISCUSSION QUESTIONS

1. How is it possible to define destination attractiveness and destination competitiveness?

2. What two major analytical frameworks have been established to understand global competitiveness?

3. What are the major limitations of these models?

4. Why is defining and measuring the concept of competitiveness such a complex and difficult task?

5. What dimensions of tourism competitiveness can be identified?

6. How might some of these conceptual factors and variables be measured?

APPLICATION

Attempt to produce a series of Key Performance Indicators that might be used to assess the competitive performance of an airline

What difficulties might be experienced in applying such an approach to Civil Aviation?

RECOMMENDED READING

Buzzell, Robert D and Bradley T Gale (1987), *The PIMS Principles: Linking Strategy to Performance*, The Free Press, New York.

Evans, N et al (2005) Strategic Management for Travel and Tourism, Elsevier.

Glaister, Keith (1991), "International Success: Company Strategy and National Advantage", *European Management Journal*, Vol. 9, No. 3 (September), 334-338.

Haahti, Antti J (1986), "Finland's Competitive Position as a Destination", *Annals of Tourism Research*, Vol. 13, 11-35.

Moutinho L (2000) Strategic Management in Travel & Tourism, Butterworth-Heineman.

Porter, M E (1990), *The Competitive Advantage of Nations*, The McMillan Press, London.

Ritchie, J R, Brent and Michel Zins (1978), "Culture as a Determinant of Attractiveness of a Tourism Region", *Annals of Tourism Research*, (April/June), 252-267.

Ritchie J R, Brent and Geoffrey I Crouch (1993) "Competitiveness in International Tourism: A Framework for Understanding and Analysis", in *Proceedings of the 43rd Annual Congress of the International Association of Scientific Experts in Tourism (AIEST)*, Argentina, October, 1993.

Stonehouse, G (2002) Business Strategy: an Introduction, Butterworth-Heineman

WEF (2006), *The World Competitiveness Report, World Economic Forum*, IMD International, Lausanne, Switzerland

CHAPTER 4

Approaches to Tourism Policy Formulation

CHAPTER OUTLINE

Introduction

Developing a framework for policy formulation

Policy outputs

The structure and composition of tourism policy

- A philosophy
- A tourism vision
- The tourism mission
- A statement of objectives and constraints
- The formulation of strategies
- The establishment of an organisational structure

Policy formulation and analysis

The process of policy formulation

- The definitional phase
- The analytical phase
- The operational phase
- The implementation phase
- The monitoring and evaluation phase

Crafting tourism policy

Summary

CHAPTER OUTCOMES

Having read this chapter and undertaken the necessary study activities, you will understand:

- The underlying characteristics of tourism policy
- The different types of tourism policy
- The structure and composition of tourism policy
- How tourism policy is formulated
- How tourism policy is crafted

INTRODUCTION

It is the intention of this chapter to develop a framework for the formulation and implementation of a national, regional or local tourism policy and its associated strategies.

To this end, the chapter will discuss the critical characteristics of a tourism policy. It will examine the structure and composition of a typical tourism policy and identify the constraints on tourism policy objectives. The process of tourism policy formulation and analysis will be examined with a view to determining how tourism policy is crafted.

DEVELOPING A FRAMEWORK FOR POLICY FORMULATION

There has been little effort devoted to the development of formal frameworks for the formulation analysis and implementation of tourism policy. To date much of the literature has come from the emerging field of the policy sciences (e.g. Johnson and Thomas 2000, Dredge and Jenkins 2007).

Ricthie (1997) has hypothesised that any policy in tourism should be characterised by:

1. A general societal consensus of the direction in which tourism development should proceed.

2. It should take a long term perspective.

3. It should concentrate on how critical and limited resources can best respond to perceived tourist needs and opportunities.

4. It should include tacit knowledge and personal experience as well as more conventional sources of information i.e. books, surveys, research reports.

5. Tourism policy should encourage and stimulate organised creativity.

6. It should be a dynamic social process i.e. ever changing and responding to different opportunities and constraints.

7. Tourism policy should allow for inputs from multiple sources and break down the traditional boundaries between disciplines.

8. Tourism policy should reflect the wider social and economic policies of the nation or region.

In review tourism policy formulation may be characterised as a dynamic social process within which an intellectual process is imbedded.

Study Activity 1

Take any given policy initiative drawn from the tourism industry and explain how it conforms to one (or all) of the aforementioned criteria.

POLICY OUTPUTS

As we have seen tourism policy involves a:

"Collection of rules, regulations, guidelines and directives .... which provide a framework within which collective and individual decisions affecting tourism development and daily activities within the industry are taken."   *Ritchie (1997)*

These rules and regulations can be found within individual companies or organisations (mirco policy - sometimes referred to as corporate strategy) and at different geographical units (or scales) of analysis vis local, regional or national tourism tourism policy.

In Europe this scale of policy analysis can be taken one step further with the development and implementation of trans-national i.e. Pan-European policy directives. These invariably emanate from the European Union. Here the concept of "mega-policy" might best be applied. Ritchie refers to mega-policy as specific major actions or patterns of actions i.e. European Economic Policy or European Transport Policy et al which can be used to attain the objectives of a tourism system.

In this context mega-policy involves the determination of the postures, assumptions and guidelines to be followed by specific tourism policies. It is a master policy, in much the same way as in the UK the policies of Visit Britain are clearly distinct from the detailed discrete policies governing the transport sector of the tourism industry.

With the EU, lack of a discrete tourism policy makes the concept of a tourism mega-policy hard to conceptualise. Tourism comes under (and is responsible to) no fewer than ten directorates. In this context perhaps the term is sometimes best applied to national (or nation state) policy guidelines. These are directly based upon and are derived from the policies which direct the total socio-economic system of the nation. They also provide the basis upon which a tourism philosophy is derived.

Study Activity 2

Aim to provide two examples of tourism mega-policy.

How do these policies conform to Ritchie's criteria?

THE STRUCTURE AND COMPOSITION OF TOURISM POLICY

Tourism policy can be conceptualised as an integrated set of components. This is illustrated in Figure 4.1.

Figure 4.1

Steps in Devising a Tourism Policy

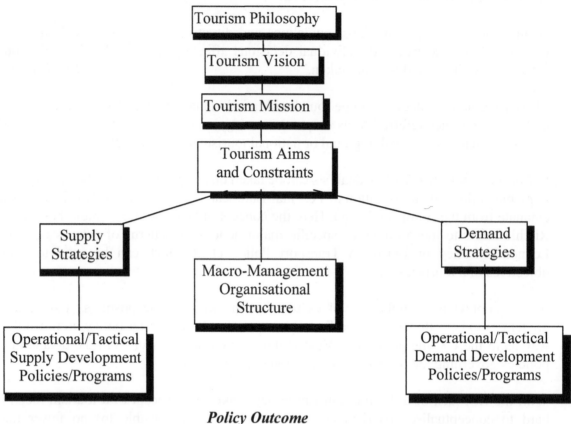

Policy Outcome

Philosophy

Philosophy may be defined as:

"a system for guiding life; as a body of principles of conduct, beliefs or traditions. It is the broad general principles of a particular subject or field of activity."

Ritchie (1991) p.11.

In a tourism context a tourism philosophy might be defined as:

A general principle or set of principles which indicate the beliefs and values of members of a society concerning how tourism shall serve the population of a country or region and which act as a guide for evaluating the utility of tourism related activities.

Any policy is derived and based upon the policies which direct the total socio-economic system of a given nation or region in which the tourism sub-system of a given nation or region is located. These principles (or philosophy) guide what can be achieved or what is possible.

44

Study Activity 3

What do you believe is the tourism philosophy of the national government (i.e. what are its values or beliefs)?

In which policy document (or documents) are these beliefs outlined?

A Tourism Vision

Any tourism policy incorporates a tourism vision. Tourism vision is an abstract view of the future of "what could be". It is a broad target to aim for. It is a prescription for the future rather than a forecast.

Tourism vision is derived through a creative process of capturing the foresight and imagination of individuals with the ability to verbalise a vision of what directions tourism could develop in the future. It is a prescription for success and focuses efforts now and in the years to come.

Study Activity 4

What vision does the national tourism office have of tourism in the country?

The Tourism Mission

Vision is reflected in the mission statement for any town, region, country or organisation.

A mission statement is

"an explicit statement of the purpose which (tourism) development or a company or organisation should serve". *Ritchie (1991) p.12*

The role of the tourism mission statement is to facilitate a general philosophy (of tourism) into specific operational objectives.

Mission statements can be simple or complex. They must neither be too broad or too narrow so as to prevent inflexibility and lost opportunities.

Study Activity 5

What is the mission statement of Visit London?

A Statement of Aims and Constraints

Any tourism policy will include a statement of what it hopes to achieve i.e. its aims.

Aims are a statement(s) of the specific results that a town, region, country or organisation hopes to achieve in a given time frame.

Tourism aims should incorporate the following characteristics:

- They should clearly contribute to the fulfilment of the mission statement.

- Measure the extent to which desired results have or have not been attained.

- Indicate future goals and desired results.

- Indicate an order of priority among multiple objectives.

- Specify a given time period.

- Be quantifiable.

- Be reasonable and achievable.

In addition to specifying those events or results which we wish to bring about, tourism aims may also specify goals which they do not want to happen as a consequence of certain actions or activities. Examples include the avoidance of environmental and cultural pollution.

The Formulation of Objectives or Strategies

Strategies are major actions or patterns of action over time for the attainment of the aims of tourism in a town, region, country or organisation.

Strategies may be either **supply** or **demand** orientated.

In a tourism context, **supply strategies** are related to:

- Physical resources;
- Human resources; or
- Financial resources.

Physical resources fundamentally determine the attractiveness of a tourism destination. They fall into nine major categories (Table 4.1). The ability of the tourism policy maker to improve the desirability of a destination increases as one moves from natural features to the determination of pricing strategy.

Table 4.1   Determinants of Attractiveness of a Tourism Destination

Component	Elements
Natural Features	Which include the general topography: flora and fauna; proximity to lakes, rivers and sea; mountains, island; hot and mineral water springs; waterfalls; as well as: amount of sunshine; temperature; winds; precipitation; discomfort index.
Culture and Social Characteristics	Which includes language; traditions; gastronomic practices; art; sculpture; music; architecture; work; religion; education; dress; leisure behaviour; history; museums; and festivals.
General Infrastructure	Which includes: fresh water supply system, electricity, road network, sewage system, telecommunications, etc...
Advanced General Infrastructure	Which includes; basic needs of civilised life such as: hospitals, chemists, banks.
Basic Services Infrastructure	Which includes; shopping places, hairdressers, food provision stores, administrative offices (police civil authority, courts, etc...) tobacconists, drug stores, opticians, newspaper kiosks, bookshops, garages, for car maintenance, gas stations, etc.

Tourism Superstructure	Residential tourism plant: hotels, motels, pensions, furnished flats, furnished rooms with private individuals, social tourism establishments (holidays, villages, camping areas, caravaning sites, youth hostels, etc) catering establishments (restaurants, taverns, self-service, grill, rooms, etc...)
	
	Receptive tourist plant:
	• For organisation of travel
	  travel agents
	  rent-a-car
	  excursions and sightseeing agents, etc.
	• For information and promotion
	  Tourists information offices at points of entry, in the cities and resorts; local of peripheral tourist organisations; special events celebration committees.
	• Recreative and sportive plant
	  Sporting facilities for winter and summer, land and sea sporting facilities and equipment, as well as theatres, movies, casinos, night clubs, tea rooms, etc.

Access and Transport Facilities	Which includes the physical distance to the region; the time involved in reaching the region; and practical barriers due to customs and security inspections as well as airports, ports for countries bordering the sea, rivers or multinational lakes, railroads and other land transport means, boats, air transport, mountain transport system, etc.
Attitudes Towards Tourists	Which involves the warmth of reception by local population; ease of communication; willingness to provide information; and a lack of hostility towards tourism activities.
Price Levels	Which involves the value received for money spent on major services, food, lodging and transportation within the region.

Source: adapted from Gearing et al (2004).

Human resources represent the second major category of supply resources. When formulating supply strategies in tourism, consideration of the following resources are necessary:

1. Quantity: the number of persons in an area wishing to work in tourism

2. Quality: technical and professional competence of personnel

3. Mix of Personnel: distribution of available tourism personnel in terms of quantity and quality

Financial resource planning is the final major component of developing a tourism supply strategy. It implies developing strategies designed to secure capital to implement a given policy. Typically financial decisions concern the following:

1. The Amount of Capital: dependent on the size and scope of the actions planned

2. Sources of Capital: the extent to which private, public, or foreign funding is sought

3. Conditions: length of borrowing, debt to equity mix

Study Activity 6

Go back to any of the tourism policy documents you have been able to identify. What, if any, supply orientated strategies do they advocate?

Tourism policy may also include **demand orientated strategies** geared towards the development of a product/destination.

Demand strategies are concerned with decisions in two main areas:

1. The establishing of targets re: markets, market demand and market segments.
2. The nature and structure of development activities.

These typically focus on four types of decision:

(i) The total level of demand development activity that is necessary or that can be supported i.e. the capacity of a programme.

(ii) The appropriate mix of demand management activities within each market vis: direct sales techniques or through an intermediary.

(iii) The most effective allocation of total funds across the various market segments.

(iv) The most appropriate timing of demand development efforts within each segment e.g. brochure launch.

Implicit in the development of demand and/or supply strategies is that a series of operational or tactical development policies and programs will evolve. Taken together they represent part of a wider overall or master policy.

Study Activity 7

Having identified some supply strategies now try and find some examples of tourism demand strategies. What do they propose?

The Establishment of an Organisational Structure

Clearly some entity within the tourism system must be designated with the responsibility for insuring that tourism policy (or policies) are co-ordinated, implemented and evaluated. The designation of such units or organisations are important elements in the structure and organisation of tourism policy.

Whatever the nature of the organisation, it must be constituted in a manner that provides it with certain key characteristics. Among these are:

1.   it must be clearly identifiable as the organisation responsible for coordinating and directing the efforts of the many parts of the diverse and complex tourism system.

2.   it must command the support of all important sectors and all majors actors in the tourism system.

3.   it must be capable of influencing the decisions and actions of the many public sector agencies/private sector departments which impact directly on the nature and quality of tourism.

4.   it must possess the tools necessary to stimulate or discourage the type and amount of supply development which is required by the overall tourism policy.

5.   it must be sufficiently independent and flexible to develop innovative strategies which can be implemented in a timely manner in response to rapidly evolving environmental conditions.

Given the above requirements, it becomes evident that the most effective organisational form in the public sector is generally considered to be an independent ministry of tourism. In cases where such a ministry does not exist, the explanation usually derives from two main sources. It may be that tourism is a relatively unimportant economic factor in the country/region in question and as such does not merit the expenditure of funds necessary to support an independent ministry. In these cases, tourism policy and development responsibilities are commonly subsumed within some larger ministry such as economic development, parks and recreation, or even cultural affairs. The second major reason why a ministry does not exist may reflect the political philosophy of the country or region. In certain countries, notably the United States, the diversity of the country and the existence of relatively strong private sector associations in tourism has led to a low level of public sector leadership with respect to policy development. In addition, this situation appears to be strongly enhanced by a lower level of government regulation of both supply and demand development activities than is found in many countries.

It is interesting to note that few, if any, countries/regions have experimented with more novel forms of organisation lying somewhat between the public and the private model. For example, the public corporation has been used in a number of countries/regions to direct and coordinate national/provincial efforts in such diverse fields as air service, petroleum development, postal services, rural services, venture development and hydro-electric power. The important common characteristics of all these fields are: most are primarily involved in the provision of services rather than the manufacture of products, most depend heavily on the use of public or natural resources, and all must satisfy some minimum standards of economic performance. Given this observation, it may be that some form of public corporation would prove effective as the leader/catalyst of tourism policy in particular countries or regions.

POLICY FORMULATION AND ANALYSIS

The Process of Policy Formulation

The process contains eleven distinct stages grouped into five main phases.

These phases are:

(i)   The definitional phase
(ii)   The analytical phase
(iii)   The operational phase
(iv)   The implementation phase
(v)   The monitoring and evaluation phase

(i)   **The definitional phase**

The definitional phase of tourism policy formulation is concerned with the development of explicit statements which define the content and direction of tourism policy.

This phase:

* Defines the nature and structure of the entity i.e. it outlines the tourism system - what it is policy-makers propose to manage.

* It explicates tourism philosophy.

* States the tourism mission.

* Determines tourism objectives and constraints.

(ii)   **The Analytical Phase**

"The analytical phase requires fundamental, value-based decisions concerning the nature and direction of tourism policy in a region". *Ritchie (1991) p.21*

The analytical phase of tourism policy formulation is composed of two sub-processes.

* Internal/supply analysis - consisting of a review and analysis of existing policies and programs regarding the development of various component sectors of the tourism industry and a resource audit which provides a comprehensive cataloguing of the quality, quantity and distribution of tourism attractions, facilities and services.

50

- <u>An external/demand analysis</u> consisting of:

   (a)   **A review of macro-level environmental/market data**

         This aims to describe the overall nature and structure of current and potential tourism demand.

   (b)   **The study of micro level environmental/market data**

         This aims to provide a motivational understanding of the behaviour of tourism markets.

   (c)   **An overview of supportive and competitive programs and policies**

Various methods can be employed to collect data needed during the analytical phase. In addition to the analysis of existing (published) data frequently used methodologies include:

- The use of public forums or "open houses".
- Focus group sessions.
- Nominal group interviews.
- The monitoring of resident/industry views.
- Community/industry "visioning" processes.
- And interest based negotiation.

Methodological frameworks for the collection and analysis of data can be 'top-down' or 'bottom-up'. Further details are outlined in Chapter 7.

(iii)   **The Operational Phase**

During this phase specific strategies and action plans are developed. The operational phase contains three conceptually different types of activity; in reality these activities are executed almost simultaneously.

The three different types of activity include:

(a)   **Identification of strategic conclusions**

      i.e. synthesising the large amounts of information obtained in the analytical phase into a limited number of major conclusions.

(b)   **The drawing of the implications of conclusions for demand/supply strategies**

      This involves a high degree of judgement on the part of individuals involved in this process. The goal of this process is to attempt to assess the significance of each conclusion for tourism - whether it be its development, organisation or nature of the product.

      While the factual conclusions of (a) may be clear, the implications of these facts for the kinds of policies needed to deal with them involves a considerable level of interpretative skills derived from both experience and a creative mind.

(c)   **Establishing policy recommendations**

In reality a range of policy options would normally be developed which attempt to respond to alternative implications or alternative scenarios. Some judgement would then be exercised as to the implications or scenarios most likely to occur. Policy recommendations most appropriate to the most likely events would then be adopted.

(iv)   **The Implementation Phase**

During this phase policy recommendations are implemented. It is important that these are on-time and within budget.

(v)   **The Monitoring and Evaluation Phase**

This phase is used:

- To assess whether objectives are being met; and
- To determine if constraints are being violated.

The purpose of monitoring is to detect possible problems early so that corrections to policies and associated strategies can be modified when required.

Study Activity 8

Now put it all together. Choose a piece of corporate strategy e.g. the marketing policy of a national airline.

What has influenced this policy? (philosophy)
What is the marketing vision?
How is both the vision and philosophy influenced by the company mission?
What are the aims of the policy?
How will these aims be achieved i.e. the strategies
Who has compiled the policy? (What is the organisational structure and how will the policy be implemented?)

THE 'CRAFTING' OF TOURISM POLICY

Mintzberg (1997) has advocated the concept of 'policy crafting'. The ensuing discussion has seen policy formulation as a rational, systematic analysis that formulates courses of action according to a specific schedule. 'Crafting' however assumes that formulation and implementation merge into a fluid process of learning through which creative policies and strategies can evolve.

In crafting strategy, the craftsperson (or people) of an organisation must know the organisations capabilities as well as its strategic direction. Like a potter the corporate strategist molds policy from past corporate capabilities and future market opportunities; together with an intimate knowledge of the material at hand.

Mintzberg assumes that policies can form as well as be formulated. A policy can emerge in response to an evolving situation, or it can be brought about deliberately, through a process of formulation followed by implementation.

Crafting assumes strategic learning. Once policy has been formulated strategic learning (i.e. evaluation, review and modification) can take place at any level in an organisation. One of the greatest fallacies in tourism policy formulation to date has been that policy should be created far removed from the details of running an organisation on a daily basis.

Finally crafting assumes the ability to strategically re-orientate policy in response to change in the external business environment. In doing so companies or organisations continually reconcile the forces of stability and change. The result may be revolutionary turmoil in the organisation to regain stability, or if the organisation does not respond quick enough, it could ultimately fail.

Study Activity 8

Here you might like to review the ever changing policies or corporate strategy of a company like British Airways. How has it lurched between revolutionary turmoil and stability since its privatisation in the early 1980s? To what aspects of the external business environment can these shifts in policy be attributed?

To manage policy is to craft thought and action, control and learning, stability and change. Mintzberg's view of the policy-maker is one of a pattern recogniser, a learner - who manages a process in which visions can emerge as well as be deliberately conceived.

SUMMARY

This chapter has attempted to draw upon existing literature in order to develop a conceptual framework for the formulation, analysis, implementation and evaluation of tourism policy. This conceptual framework has described the structure of tourism policy and discussed the nature of its major components. It has also outlined the process of policy formulation.

The chapter has asserted that tourism policy can be analysed at different spatial (or organisational) scales of analysis. At its most basic this relates to a series of actions initiated by different sectors of the tourism industry. At the other extreme is what Ritchie terms 'megapolicy' or a tourism policy that recognises and supports the socio-economic well being of the citizens of an entire country or countries.

Any conceptual model is clearly idealistic in its scope and content. This has been recognised by Mintzberg. While much work remains to be done to refine concepts and ideas, the models presented in this chapter provide guidelines for policy-makers faced with the task of allocating scarce resources in an ever changing world.

DISCUSSION QUESTIONS

1.   How can the study of political science enhance the study of tourism policy?

2.   Outline the underlying characteristics or assumptions of any tourism policy.

3.   How might tourism policy be regarded as a dynamic social process?

4.   What is meant by the term tourism 'megapolicy'?

5.   Who has responsibility for developing tourism policy in the European Union? Why might tourism policy in the EU be regarded as being fragmented?

6.   How can the structure and composition of tourism policy be conceptualised as an integrated set of components?

7.   Distinguish between a tourism mission and tourism policy objectives.

8.   Why might an independent management organisation (like a regional or national tourist board) prove to be the most successful method of implementing a tourism policy?

9.   Outline the process of policy formulation according to Ritchie (1997).

10.   Why is it necessary to monitor tourism policy?

11.   How can tourism policy be said to be 'crafted'?

APPLICATION

In your view what are the major policy issues currently facing any sector of the tourism industry? How is the sector responding to these i.e. what is its strategic response?

RECOMMENDED READING

Dredge, D and Jenkins J (2007) Tourism Planning and Policy, Wiley.

Mintzberg, H (1997) Crafting Strategy. Harvard Business Review. July-August.

Mintzberg H (1998) The Strategy Process – Concepts Contexts and Cases, Prentice Hall

Johnson, P and Thomas B (2000) Perspectives on Tourism Policy, Chapter 13, Mansell

Ritchie, J R Brent (1991) Tourism Policy and Strategy - Structure and Process. Travel Research Association of Canada, Banff, Alberta.

Ritchie, J.R. Brent (1997) Developing a Tourism Mega-policy in Ritchie, J.R Brent and Goeldner C (2000) Tourism Principles and Practice, Wiley

CHAPTER 5

Stakeholder Involvement

CHAPTER OUTLINE

Introduction

The stakeholder group concept

Stakeholder groups

- Business as an interest group

- Labour organisations

- Special interest groups

Stakeholder networks

The significance of stakeholder groups in tourism policy making

Stakeholder power in tourism policy making

Conclusion

CHAPTER OBJECTIVES

Having read this chapter and undertaken the necessary study activities you should understand:

- What is a stakeholder group?

- The features which characterise stakeholder groups.

- The types of stakeholders found in the policy making process.

- How stakeholders can influence tourism policy making.

- The concept of the 'stakeholder network'.

- The relationship between politics, policy and stakeholder power in tourism policy making.

- How stakeholders can set their own policy making agendas.

- How stakeholder power is relatively dispersed in the policy arena.

INTRODUCTION

Stakeholders seek to influence the tourism policy making process. Because individuals, by themselves, can only assert a certain degree of influence on tourism policy-making it is not unusual for them to come together to form blocs of interests or 'interest groups'.

Since the Second World War there has been a tremendous expansion in the number and scope of interest groups in the policy making process. Up until the 1960s, interest groups were primarily business-association based. However, since the early 1960s, there has been rapid growth in Western nations in the number of citizen and public interest groups, particularly in the area of consumer and environmental concerns.

Tourism policy making has not been immune from the growth in interest groups. Until the mid-1960s, tourism-related interest groups were generally confined to industry and professional associations. However, the growth of consumer and environmental organisations extended the number of groups who had an interest in tourism issues, particularly as they related to aspects of tourism development at the local level. In the 1980s and the early 1990s, the range of groups was extended still further as social issues, often in relation to developing countries, and international trade became significant and, in terms of the latter, more pervasive. Therefore, it is important to realise that stakeholder interest groups go well beyond those which are part of the tourism industry and include a vast array of community, public and special interest groups.

Stakeholder groups are an integral component of the tourism policy making process. To this end this chapter outlines the nature of the stakeholder group concept and details the crowded and highly complex policy making environment within which stakeholder groups operate.

THE STAKEHOLDER GROUP CONCEPT

The term 'stakeholder group' tends to be used interchangeably with the terms 'pressure group' or 'organised interest group'. A stakeholder can be defined as any individual or organisation which makes a claim, either directly or indirectly on decision makers so as to influence policy.

Several features characterise stakeholders.

- Their motives can be political/non-political.

- They seek to influence policy directly or indirectly e.g. through the conduct of public relations campaigns or disrupting public forums.

- While sometimes cast in a negative light (e.g. environmental groups in ski field areas) their value to policy formulation cannot be under-estimated.

Stakeholders operate on a number of different scales vis: local, regional, national or international. They can be highly, relatively and non-institutionalised in orientation.

Highly institutionalised stakeholder groups are characterised by having access to a whole range of resources, a high level of credibility in bargaining and negotiating with policy makers and an organised membership. Business organisations and labour organisations are typical of this particular type of stakeholder group.

Non-institutionalised stakeholder groups are characterised by their limited degree of organisational permanence, as they will likely disappear altogether once their interests have been achieved or have been rendered unattainable.

Hall (2000) illustrates the various types of institutionalised stakeholder groups that occur at different scales in the tourism policy making process (Table 5.1).

Table 5.1   Tourism Stakeholder Groups

Scale	Highly Institutionalised		Relatively Institutionalised	Non-institutionalised
International	World Travel & Tourism Council		Environmental and social organisations, e.g. Tourism Concern, International Union for the Conservation of Nature and Natural Resources (IUCN), World Wildlife Fund	Occasional environmental or social issues, often location specific, e.g. campaign to End Child Prostitution in Asian Tourism (ECPAT), or campaign to end golf course development in South-East Asia
National	National tourism industry associations, trade unions, national professional and trade associations		Environmental and consumer organisations, e.g. National Trust, the Wilderness Society, Sierra Club	Single-issue environmental groups, e.g. those opposing airport development
Local	Chambers of Commerce, regional tourism business associations		Rate-payers and resident associations	Groups opposed to tourist development in a specific location, e.g. anti-resort development groups, Olympic Bread and Circus coalitions

Stakeholder groups can be very diverse in their understanding of resources, methods and effectiveness in the policy making process. They also work in a highly crowded and complex policy environment. The diffuse nature of the tourism industry and of tourism policy means that stakeholders can have very different policy objectives and place different sets of demands on tourism policy.

There remains a wide array of groups that seek to have their goals satisfied in the policy making process. These include business groups, planning teams, environmentalists and local residents (to name just a few).

STAKEHOLDER GROUPS

BUSINESS AS AN INTEREST GROUP

One of the key issues in understanding the tourism policy process is identifying the role of business interests in determining policy. Despite the growth of public interest, consumer, environmental and community-based organisations in the last two decades, Schlozman (1984: 1029) argues that 'the pressure system is tilted heavily in favour of the well-off, especially business'. The perception that business dominates policy making has been a major concern for students of the policy process over the years. One of the strongest accounts of the business-government relationship comes from American political scientist Charles Lindblom.

Lindblom (1977) argued that in all private enterprise market-oriented societies, business occupies a privileged position in the policy process. Business performance affects employment, prices, inflation, production, growth and the material standard of living, which are items utilised by government at all levels to measure success. Therefore, government leadership may well be strongly influenced by business leadership in order to achieve certain policy goals. Indeed, Craik (1990: 29) observed that 'the private sector claims that because it takes risks, it should shape policy'. Nevertheless, as she went on to note, 'the fostering of the private sector inevitably leads to charges of clientelism, the coincidence between policy outcomes and the interests of key lobbyists'.

According to Lindblom (1977) a common tacit understanding exists between business and policy makers in Western economies in terms of the general conditions necessary for profitable private enterprise operations.

Lindblom argues that business not only controls the agenda but also engages in interest group activity to supplement its privileged position. Of those secondary issues that are contested by others, such as trade unions and environmental groups, business interest group activity is regarded as being much more effective than that of its rivals in the policy making process. Business wins proportionately in policy debates with other interest groups because, while other interests compete using their members' own incomes and energies, business is able to use corporate resources, thereby giving business a triple advantage - in funds, organisation and access.

Affiliation in general business associations and trade associations amplifies the organised voice of business. Lindblom believes that business's privileged position is widely accepted because business has shaped citizens' beliefs through workplace socialisation and ownership of the media. Primary issues are not raised because the people have been persuaded that the issues are discouragingly complex, not worth their energy, or that agitation is bad or unlikely to succeed.

Although it is clear that business has a major influence on tourism policy, it should be noted that business does not always speak with a unified voice. Given the co-ordination problems posed by the partial industrialisation of the tourism industry noted above, tourism businesses may well be in disagreement over policy positions. For example, a nature-based tourism operation may well be in support of declaring an area a national park with a low degree of visitor access, whereas a mass tourist business operation may prefer the area being developed as a golf course or theme park with high visitor access. Furthermore, there may be differences in objectives between tourism corporations and organisations in different industry sectors and different industry representative organisations, while conflict between business organisations may also occur on an inter-regional scale.

Having resources is not the same as mobilising them to wield successful political influence. In the tourism policy arena this is particularly the case in the conservation area, where there is widespread public support in Western countries for environmental protection measures. Business associations may use advocacy advertising in an effort to create a basis of support in the community for industry actions and positions. Where there is opposition to tourism development by local communities and/or conservation organisations, tourism businesses will often refer to the perceived economic and employment benefits of tourism.

LABOUR ORGANISATIONS

The tourism industry labour force has had a history of low unionisation. This is, in major part, because of the highly seasonal, part-time and casual nature of employment in the tourism industry which is related to a high level of voluntary labour turnover and minimal on-the-job training (Shaw and Williams 1994; Hall 1995). The low levels of unionisation in the tourism industry gives trade unions little leverage in negotiations with business and correspondingly little influence as an interest group in the tourism policy making process at the macro-level.

SPECIAL INTEREST GROUPS

Special interest groups vis:- public interest groups, consumer groups, conservation groups, and social justice groups - have had a dramatic impact on tourism policy making over the last few years. The relatively high position of issues of sustainability on the contemporary tourism policy agenda is due in no small part to the activities of environmental groups, such as Greenpeace (international), World Wildlife Fund (international), the Sierra Club (United States and Canada), the National Trust (United Kingdom, Australia) and various national park and wilderness organisations Although environmental organisations have traditionally only had an indirect involvement in tourism policy, their advocacy on conservation issues has been a part of the general policy environment within which tourism operates. For example, conservation groups seeking to establish a national park and exclude non-compatible land uses will often use tourism as part of the economic arguments for park creation.

In recent years, however, tourist groups have taken a more direct interest in tourism as the size and scale of tourism has increasingly come to impact negatively on the natural environment (Williams 2004). Furthermore, the growth of ecotourism as a tourism marketing category has meant that conservation organisations have become active in monitoring, promoting or even establishing nature-based tourism operations, particularly in developing countries. Conservation and environmental interest groups are therefore playing a substantial role in tourism policy making at both the national and international levels and are increasingly finding themselves being drawn into the institutional structure of policy making. For example, Greenpeace was invited on to the planning team for the Sydney 2000 Olympics bid in order to assist in the promotion of the Games as a 'Green' event.

Although conservation interest groups are the major form of non-producer interest group, social justice groups are also increasingly starting to influence tourism policy. Two major types of social justice groups may be identified: native peoples' interest groups which seek either the economic benefits of tourism or to restrict tourism's impacts; or broad based social justice groups which are attempting to develop fair and responsible tourism trade. In the latter category, the British organisation Tourism Concern is slowly starting to impact on tourism policy making, although its political strength relative to that of the wider tourism industry is minute.

The majority of special interest stakeholder groups operate at the local level. Most are established in relation to tourism development issues and are primarily resident action groups. By virtue of being single-issue groups they tend to have few resources and will only be able to sustain action for a short period of time.

One of the characteristics of special interest stakeholder groups is their association with what is known as the NIMBY syndrome. NIMBY stands for 'Not In My Backyard' and refers to situations in which although there may be in principle agreement for a particular policy in a community, e.g. tourism development or the development of tourism related infrastructure such as transport links or improved sewage disposal services, the community or group of residents do not want the development in their neighbourhood. Apart from resort development, excellent examples of NIMBY include the location of airports (we want to fly but we don't want to live under the flight path) and the construction of stadia (we want to support the team but we don't want the noise and traffic problems).

NIMBY poses particularly difficult problems for policy makers. Although tourism NIMBY groups are typically not of the same scale as, say, the siting of a nuclear reactor or intractable waste dumps, they will have the capacity to cause a great deal of turbulence in the policy making process, particularly for local government. (Witness the protests against a third runway at London Heathrow Airport in August 2007). Therefore, the ability of special-interest groups to resist unpopular siting decisions by government or the private sector will typically depend on their level of organisation, sophistication, and ability to generate wider support from other elements of the policy making process for their cause.

STAKEHOLDER NETWORKS

The proliferation of interests in the policy process over the past two decades has not only increased the number of stakeholders prepared to participate in policy making, but has also made the process more complex. Within the policy arena is found a voluntary and fluid configuration of people with varying degrees of commitment to a particular cause.

The concept of stakeholder networks is important for an understanding of policy formation, and agenda building in particular, because it provides insight into the critical processes which frequently determine the definition of policy issues and the articulation of policy alternatives. Alliances are formed between stakeholder groups and shift depending on the issues and the outcomes involved. Where network participants coalesce to advocate for particular policies, an advocacy coalition can be said to have emerged (Sabatier 1987). However, within the tourism policy making system the creation of advocacy coalitions is becoming increasingly difficult. Coalitions require a critical mass of supporters to lead to action and the increasing complexity of the tourism policy arena works against coalition as the number of stakeholders has increased.

As Cigler observes:

> "It has become more difficult to practice consensual politics due to changes in the nature of public policy, structural reforms in the policy process, and the impact of the public interest movement, which has brought a number of actors into the process who are willing to utilise 'outsider' strategies and has introduced electoral costs for legislators unwilling to pay attention to broader interests ... Many issues have been redefined ... policies are not characterised by compromise, accommodation and secrecy. Rather, they involve confrontation, a wider scope of conflict, and, often, more public scrutiny."

> (Cigler 1991: 122)

THE SIGNIFICANCE OF STAKEHOLDER GROUPS IN TOURISM POLICY MAKING

Incorporation, by which a stakeholder group is co-opted into the formal policy making structures of decision makers is a common response to interest-group demands. For example, environmental groups might be invited to sit on the boards of natural resource management agencies or recreational organisations might be invited to join the management advisory committees of national parks.

> "this co-operation between groups and decision makers can sometimes be a good thing. But it may sometimes be a very bad thing. These groups, use to each other's needs, may become increasingly preoccupied with each other, insensitive to the needs of outsiders, and impervious to new recruitment and to new ideas. Or the members of the various interest group elites may identify more and more with each other and less and less with the interests of the groups they represent"
>
> (Deutsch 1970: 56)

Deutsch (1970) argued that in highly pluralistic and organised societies in which incorporation is the norm, policy arenas become a cycle of alternating states of immobility (as a result of incorporation) and crisis (produced by new interest group demands from outside of the institutional structure). In order to have their demands incorporated into the policy making process, stakeholder groups may resort to non-conventional political tactics. For example, conservation groups throughout Western society have used direct protest actions, such as sitting in front of bulldozers and chaining themselves to trees, in order to attract media attention and therefore raise public awareness of environmental issues and their handling by government and business. Similarly, in the early 1970s, women's groups in the Philippines staged protest rallies during visits by the Japanese Prime Minister in order to draw attention to the large numbers of Japanese men travelling to the country as sex tourists. Such actions played an important role in highlighting the impacts of institutionalised prostitution in the Philippines and helped encourage legislative action on child and mail-bride prostitution (Philippine Women's Research Collective 1985). Nevertheless, while direct action may be a useful technique in gaining attention for a policy issue, it is unlikely that policy shifts will result unless group demands are supported by a wider set of community values.

The relationship between stakeholders and decision makers clearly raises questions about the extent to which established policy processes lead to outcomes which are in the 'public interest' rather than just a deal between policy makers and sectional interests. There is general agreement in Western democracies that policy makers should avoid 'client politics' in which interests seem to have a disproportionate influence on policy areas.

Equality of access is clearly crucial in assessing how far some groups have been able to influence the policy making process to their advantage. However, it is worth noting that despite the undoubted strength of business interests in determining tourism policy, there are signs that other interests are able to influence policy settings. In particular, environmental groups have performed relatively well in pushing conservation perspectives on tourism development.

Study Activity 1

Attempt to answer the following questions:

1. *How has the increased number and range of tourism-related stakeholder groups affected the policy making process?*

2. *What are the differences between a stakeholder group and a political party?*

3. *What is a stakeholder network?*

4. *To what extent is tourism policy determined by business interests rather than the public interest?*

STAKEHOLDER POWER IN TOURISM POLICY MAKING

> "Policy is deliberate coercion-statements attempting to set forth the purpose, the means, the subjects and the objects of coercion."
>
> (Lowi 1970: 314-315)

A prescriptive-rationalist approach to tourism policy would see the decisions of any organisation as being part of an inherently rational policy making process in which goals, values and objectives can be ranked and identified after the collection and systematic evaluation of necessary data. While this approach to policy making is influential (Ritchie 1992) it is also extremely misleading as it fails to recognise the inherently political nature of tourism policy. As Fischer and Forester recognise:

> "policy and planning arguments are intimately involved with relations of power and the exercise of power, including the concerns of some and excluding others, distributing responsibility as well as causality, imputing blame as well as efficacy, ,and employing particular political strategies and problem framing and not others."
>
> (Fischer and Forester 1993: 7)

Politics and policy are inextricably linked. Politics is about power, who gets what, where, how and why. Decisions affecting tourism policy, the nature of organisational involvement in tourism, the structure of tourism agencies, the nature of tourism development, and community involvement in tourism planning and policy all emerge from a political process. As noted, this process involves the values of actors (individuals, interest groups and public and private organisations) in a struggle for power.

SETTING THE TOURISM POLICY AGENDA

Political issues have an organisational aspect. As Crozier (1964: 107) noted, 'The behaviour and attitudes of people and groups within an organisation cannot be explained without reference to the power relationships existing among them.' Therefore, research on tourism policy needs to connect the substance of policy to the process of policy making including the relationship between power, structure and values. Studies of tourism policy making should therefore attempt to understand not only the politically imposed limitations upon the scope of policy and decision making, but also the political framework within which the research process itself takes place.

One of the issues which arises in the identification of the different dimensions of power is the manner in which the policy agenda may be set or framed prior to various interests being involved in policy debates.

Problems and policy alternatives can be defined before they reach the policy arena in two primary ways. First, is by way of a dominant ideology or set of values which defines the parameters within which problems are defined and discussed, and solutions conceived and carried out. This ideology may be a state or an organisational ideology.

The second means is through the setting of the rules by which policy debate is carried out, in other words, the 'rules of the game'. The 'rules of the game' are 'a set of predominant values, beliefs, rituals and institutional procedures that operate systematically and consistently to the benefit of certain persons and groups at the expense of others'. Those who benefit 'are placed in a preferred position to defend and promote their vested interests' (Bachrach and Baratz 1970: 43-44).

Therefore, institutionalised rules condition the cognitive and normative understandings of different stakeholders thereby facilitating some strategies while constraining others. Institutionalised rules refer to accepted ways of viewing how society works and consequent prescriptions for attaining objectives. For example, a parliamentary or congressional committee may be established to enquire into certain issues surrounding the tourism industry, but the terms of reference which are set by the committee will determine the scope of their policy discussions.

The challenge for groups whose interests are not met in the definition of policy alternatives is to try and change the policy agenda. Nelson (1984: 20) distinguished between three types of political agendas which are drawn up to consider matters of public policy. The first is the governmental agenda which consists of what issues government institutions are considering. The second is the popular agenda which is made up of the general public's awareness. The third is the professional agenda which is the awareness of an informed public which promotes a particular view of a specific issue. According to Michaels (1992: 242), a policy community in the form of various interest groups 'operates with a professional agenda but seeks to have their issue placed on the governmental or public agenda either directly or by using a popular agenda as a means to get the attention of decision makers'. However, such a statement assumes that the policy agenda is relatively open, and that entry to the policy making process is available to all interests. In some policy issues, particularly those relating to non-economic factors or those areas on which there is widespread public support, then this may be possible. Nevertheless, when policy issues are primarily economic in orientation, the agenda will be more closed because of the dominance of economic thinking in policy settings.

Pluralism refers to the belief that power is relatively dispersed in a society and that policy makers are open to influence by a wide range of interest groups. As a result, political decisions are reached through a process of bargaining, negotiation and compromise between the various stakeholders involved. Power is therefore diffused through a society.

In reality some stakeholder groups have more power than others. Certainly groups that are unorganised and inactive generally lack the capacity and opportunity to influence decision makers in order to obtain some of their goals. Also, some stakeholder groups, particularly business groups, are demonstrably more powerful in the policy making environment.

Stakeholder groups can find bias by government in that government's may only recognise certain political viewpoints. Pluralism then is no guarantee of political openness or popular sovereignty.

Study Activity 2

Discuss why it is not always possible for public participation in tourism policy making to represent the public interest.

CONCLUSION

This chapter has indicated the nature of stakeholder groups and their prospective influence on tourism policy. It has highlighted the strength of business interests in determining tourism policy settings and the weakness of organised labour. It was also noted that special interest groups such as conservation, consumer, rate-payer, and public interest organisations are increasingly influencing tourism policy and are likely to continue to do so in the future.

Of major significance in terms of the policy process is the growing number of stakeholder groups operating in the tourism policy environment and the corresponding complexity of policy making. The complexity and number of stakeholders clearly provides a major challenge to decision makers as well, of course, as to the interest groups themselves in the achievement of their objectives and the possibility of consensual politics.

Finally the chapter emphasised the critical role that power plays in tourism policy.

Power is clearly a key element in understanding how decisions are made and why certain values are excluded from tourism policy. The challenge for many involved in tourism studies is to acknowledge the centrality of power in tourism policy, and its relationship to values, interests and institutional arrangements. In the absence of such acknowledgement, much tourism research will continue to be blind to the critical role of argument in the policy process and maintain its supposedly value-neutral appraisal of tourism policy.

RECOMMENDED READING

Cigler (1986) Interest Group Politics, 2nd edn., CQ Press, Washington DC.

Evans, N et al (2005) Strategic Management in Travel and Tourism, Chapter 1, Elsevier

Hall, C.M. (2000) Tourism and Politics: Policy Power and Place, Belhaven Press

Lindblom, C. (1980), The Policy Making Process, Prentice-Hall, New Jersey.

Lowi, T. (1970) Decision making versus policy making, Public Administration Review 30(3), pp 314-325.

Schlazman (1986) Organised Interests and American Democracy, Harper and Row, New York.

CHAPTERS 1-5 - A REVIEW

The first five chapters have concentrated on the conceptual dimensions of tourism policy and its important role in establishing a framework for the creation and management of a competitive destination or organisation.

Before we move ahead it is important that you should be able to:

- Explain why tourism policy is important, why it is needed, what it accomplishes, and how it affects both the tourism system and individual operations.

- Describe the structure and content of a tourism policy.

- Describe and explain the process of tourism policy formulation.

- Identify the factors which determine the attractiveness and competitiveness of a tourism destination.

- Describe and explain the structure and content of the Model of Destination or Organisational Competitiveness.

- Identify specific overall economic and social policies that have an impact on the competitiveness and success of a tourism destination or organisation.

- Demonstrate an understanding of how different government or private sector policies impact on the various components of the Destination or Organisational Competitiveness Model.

- Demonstrate an understanding of how different government or private sector policies impact on individual firms in the tourism sector.

- Identify the major global forces which impact on the competitiveness of a tourism destination or organisation, and to which policy makers must adapt.

- Identify the nature of the problems challenges and opportunities that these forces pose for policy makers.

- Identify the various stakeholders that are involved in the process of policy-making and how differences in political power and control can influence the policy agenda.

The first five chapters have concentrated on the conceptual dimensions of tourism policy, and its important role in establishing a framework for the creation and management of a competitive destination or organisation.

Before we move ahead it is important that you should be able to:

- Explain why tourism policy is important, why it is needed, what it accomplishes, and how it affects both the tourism system and individual operations.

- Describe the structure and content of a tourism policy.

- Describe and explain the process of tourism policy formulation.

- Identify the factors which determine the attractiveness and competitiveness of a tourism destination.

- Describe and explain the structure and content of the Model of Destination or Organisation Competitiveness.

- Identify specific overall economic and social policies that have an impact on the competitiveness and success of a tourism destination or organisation.

- Provide with an interpretation of how different government or private sector policies impact on the various components of the Destination or Organisation Competitiveness Model.

- Demonstrate an understanding of how different government or private sector policies impact on individual firms in the tourism sector.

- Identify the major global forces which impact on the competitiveness of a tourism destination or organisation and to which policy makers must adapt.

- Identify the nature and significance of challenges and opportunities that these forces pose for tourism.

- Identify the major stakeholders that are involved in the process of policy-making and the manner in which they may exert an influence on the policy agenda.

Policy and Research Activity

CHAPTER 6

Information and Research for Tourism Policy Formulation

CHAPTER OUTLINE

Introduction

The role of research in tourism managerial decision-making

Research as an information source

Identifying and classifying research needs

Towards a model of management research

The research process

- The purpose of research
- Planning research
- Key requirements for good research
- Doing research

Primary research

Secondary research

The research process - a step by step approach

Conclusion

CHAPTER OBJECTIVES

Having read this chapter and undertaken the various study activities you should:

- Be able to identify and review the nature of information and research which is required to support effective policy development

- Review the major approaches to the gathering of information for policy development and management decision-making.

INTRODUCTION

It is the intention of this chapter to review and discuss the information and research which is required to support effective policy development and to show how this information and research can be assembled or carried out. To this end the chapter will examine the role of research in tourism policy development; examine information sources and information needs; and attempt to provide an outline and understanding of the research process.

THE ROLE OF RESEARCH IN TOURISM MANAGEMENT DECISION-MAKING

Study Activity 1

What do you understand by the term research?

Study Activity 2

How might research activity support management decision-making?

The concept of research is diffused and often highly abused. While it is agreed that the term refers to some systematic form of investigation of a given topic; the nature of research can vary between any two given fields e.g. archaeology and transport economics.

Even within the field of management decision-making, research implies a wide variety of ideas and methods vis: applied, analytical, descriptive, exploratory, causal, empirical, theoretical, cross sectional and longitudinal. The challenge to managers is to choose the type of information - gathering process most relevant to each particular decision-making situation.

RESEARCH AS AN INFORMATION SOURCE

Study Activity 3

What types of information do managers need in deciding on a tourism policy/strategy for their company or organisation?

Philip Kotler (1981) views the total information needs of any company or organisation as consisting of:

(i)   Internal (Management accounting) information.

(ii)   external information - designed to monitor changing conditions in an organisation's (political, economic, social, legal et al) business environment.

(iii)   research information - providing in-depth knowledge pertaining to specific problems or situations.

The internal, external or research information needs of a company or organisation are continually changing in response to different conditions both outside and within an organisation.

IDENTIFYING AND CLASSIFYING RESEARCH NEEDS

It is possible to identify and classify the research needs of any organisation according to three major dimensions of the management process. These dimensions can be identified as:

- The level of management activity
- The stage of the management process
- The function of the management activity

(i)   **Levels of management activity**

Robert Anthony (1965) suggests that any organisation has to deal with the following management problems

- Strategic activities vis: long-term or broad scale issues that determine or change the character of any organisation. e.g. political or technical change.

- Tactical activities - associated with the on-going administration of the enterprise.

- Operational activities vis: specific actions involved in carrying out tasks.

(ii)   **The stage of the management process**

The number and identity of stages in the management process are by no means agreed upon by scholars in the field.

Ritchie (1987), for example, identifies four

- Analysis - providing an understanding of the nature of the problem.

- Planning - the setting of objectives and the evaluation of alternatives for meeting these objectives.

- Execution

- Evaluation/Control - measuring the extent to which an activity or action has achieved its original objectives.

    Objectively exploring the causes or reasons for successes or failures.

(iii)   **The function of the management activity**

The functional areas of a management organisation include the following activities:

- Finance
- Marketing
- Production
- Control
- Personnel

70

- Co-ordination

TOWARDS A MODEL OF MANAGEMENT RESEARCH

Based upon the three previously defined dimensions of the management process, it is possible to identify within the framework five broad categories of research which are used in varying degrees by different management teams when formulating policy or policies (Figure 6.1). These five categories can be referred to as:

- Operational research
- Managerial research
- Action research
- Strategic and policy research
- Evaluation research

Operational research consists primarily of a range of quantitative/analytical techniques designed to formulate and test decisions. Such techniques are prescriptive and integrate all stages of the management process. Examples of such research in tourism would include studies to determine optimal traffic flows at tourist attractions.

Managerial research covers a broad range of research types including those most commonly employed by management. Typically such research deals with an important problem of limited scope for which management has need of additional information on which to base a decision. Examples of such studies include those concerning the market potential for a new attraction, the best approach for the implementation of a new accounting system, or a feasibility study for a new hotel. In general, such research projects have one feature in common: they concern the seeking of solutions as to what should be done to solve a given problem and how to implement this solution. While there are exceptions, there are relatively few studies related to the control aspect of the management process, that is, studies which attempt to evaluate the degree of success of a given marketing activity, accounting system, or investment program. In brief, managerial research tends to be future and present oriented as opposed to taking an interest in the effectiveness of prior actions. This generalisation is reflected in Fig. 6.1.

Action research involves a continuous gathering and analysing of research data during the normal ongoing operations of an organisation or the execution of a specific management program and the simultaneous feeding of the results into the organisation so as to change its model of functioning. As such, it is seen that action research is a continuing, task-oriented form of study designed to provide continuous feedback regarding the performance of a management activity and to improve that performance through direct forms of intervention suggested by the research findings. As shown in Fig 7.1 action research is considered to be a part of the tactical level of management activity, and, because of its continuous and recursive nature, it is carried out within both the execution and control stages of the management process.

Strategic research is a more recent phenomenon insofar as its recognition as a formal field of research is concerned. As such, it is less well defined and understood. Despite this situation, two major categories of strategic research can be identified. Policy research relates to the strategic analysis and planning activities of a tourism organisation (Fig. 7.1) or the tourism system as a whole. It appears to be composed of three elements: research which studies how policy formulation occurs with a view to understanding and improving the process; research which is designed to analyse situations at the strategic level and to formulate overall policy proposals; and research which systematically evaluates the priorities to be accorded to conflicting/complementary policy alternatives. Methodologies related to actual cases of strategic analysis and policy formulation range from various forms of decision theory to the expert judgement consensus approach commonly referred to as the Delphi Method and the Nominal Group Technique (see Chapter 7). Approaches to the ordering of the attractiveness of various policy options and studying the trade-offs among them have been referred to as priority analysis.

Study Activity 4

Attempt to provide one example of the following forms of strategic research in tourism.

The Delphi Method

Nominal Group Technique

Priority Analysis

Evaluation research can be viewed as the complement of policy research in which the objectives, strategies, and programs so derived are monitored both during and after their implementation (Fig.6.1) in order to determine their degree of success and failure as well as the underlying causes of their impact.

Figure 6.1 : Classification of Research Methodologies According to Three Dimensions of the Management Process

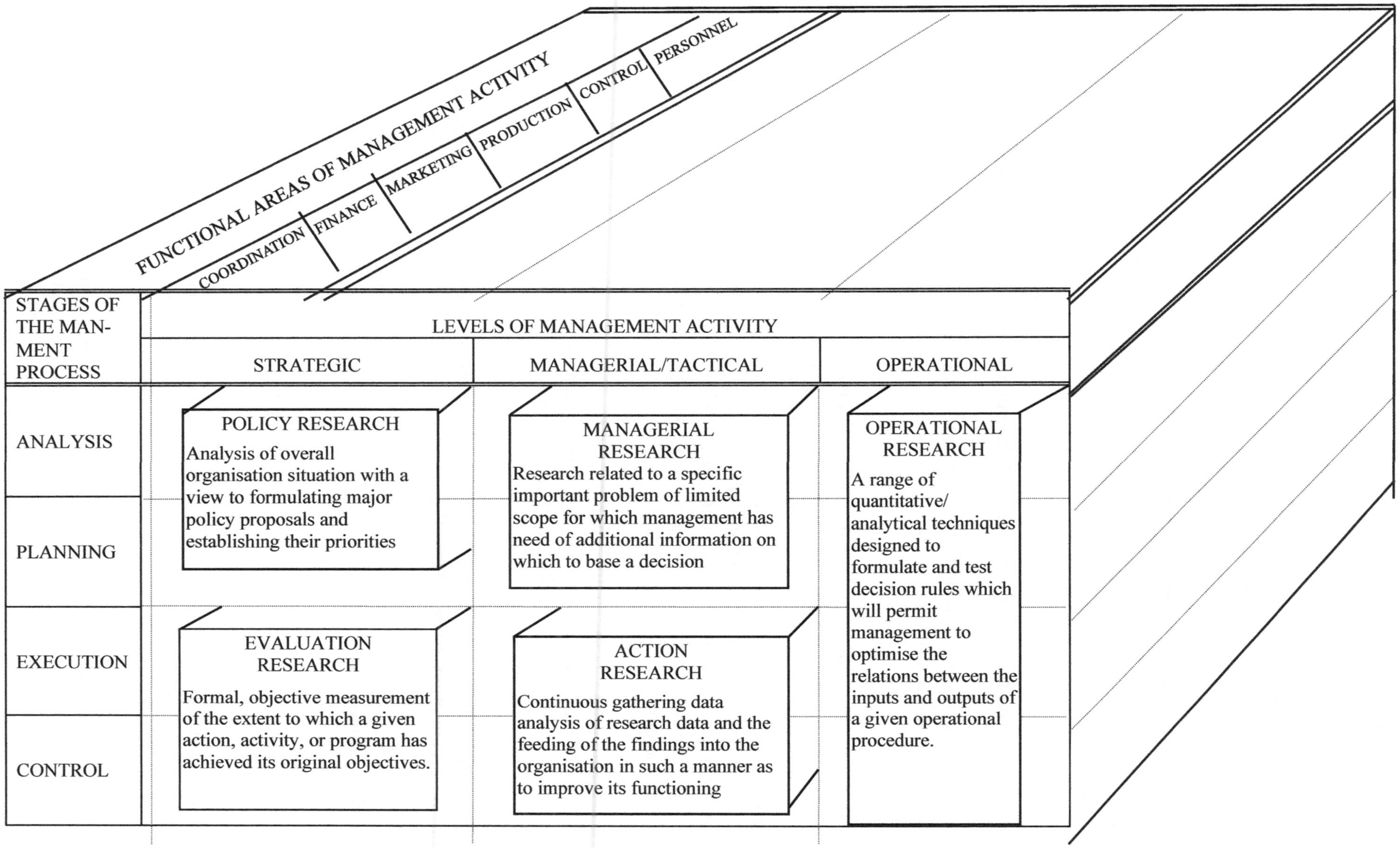

FUNCTIONAL AREAS OF MANAGEMENT ACTIVITY

COORDINATION | FINANCE | MARKETING | PRODUCTION | CONTROL | PERSONNEL

LEVELS OF MANAGEMENT ACTIVITY

STAGES OF THE MAN-MENT PROCESS	STRATEGIC	MANAGERIAL/TACTICAL	OPERATIONAL
ANALYSIS	POLICY RESEARCH — Analysis of overall organisation situation with a view to formulating major policy proposals and establishing their priorities	MANAGERIAL RESEARCH — Research related to a specific important problem of limited scope for which management has need of additional information on which to base a decision	OPERATIONAL RESEARCH — A range of quantitative/analytical techniques designed to formulate and test decision rules which will permit management to optimise the relations between the inputs and outputs of a given operational procedure.
PLANNING			
EXECUTION	EVALUATION RESEARCH — Formal, objective measurement of the extent to which a given action, activity, or program has achieved its original objectives.	ACTION RESEARCH — Continuous gathering data analysis of research data and the feeding of the findings into the organisation in such a manner as to improve its functioning	
CONTROL			

Source: Ritchie, 1994

73

IDENTIFYING RESEARCH METHODS AND DATA NEEDS

Each research category previously outlined is:

(i)   Appropriate to a particular management situation;
(ii)   Requires particular information or data;
(iii)   Utilises a specific Methodology;
(iv)   Analyses data in a particular way;
(v)   Produces specific information to assist management decide or act on a situation.

The nature of the management situation

The three different dimensions of the management process give rise to at least five different types of decision-making situations and consequently a category of research appropriate to each situation.

The type of information, data required and data analysis

Each of the five research categories has distinctly different data needs. Policy research requires primarily macro-level data. This data is often available from government sources or the private sector.

Evaluation research requires specific data related to the evaluation criteria chosen. This data must usually be collected within a specially designed project.

Management/tactical research also requires specific data relevant to a particular problem. Such data generally can be placed in one of two categories: descriptive information providing an overall understanding of the key factors involved in a given problem situation or highly precise information used for in-depth analysis of a limited number of variables influencing a particular situation.

There are similarities between the approach and needs of action research and evaluation research. However, action research strongly de-emphasises the evaluative aspects of performance measures and uses them only as guidelines to indicate problem areas and to take immediate corrective action.

Finally, operational research has highly precise information needs related to particular tasks within the organisation. Such information must normally be measured using means which provide highly accurate, reliable, and timely data.

Research Methodologies

Policy research employs at least three important types of research methodology: longitudinal studies, simulation models (designed to test the impact of alternative policy decisions) and consensus judgements

Evaluation research may employ a variety of measures and data collection methods depending on the research objective. Examples include utilisation and satisfaction surveys and comparisons with non user control groups.

With management/tactical research there exist a number of primary data collection approaches which include survey research methods, techniques of laboratory or field experimentation designed to test the effectiveness of alternative courses of action, observational methods which furnish insight into human, organisational, or functional behaviour under normal environmental conditions, and the simulation of sub-systems of an organisation.

The types of measures employed are correspondingly varied and include: technical or factual data bearing directly on the problem; measures of awareness, attitudes, and opinions; measures of effectiveness of and reaction to alternative actions; and measures describing particular aspects of behaviour which are relevant to the question at hand. In general, each of these has been the object of significant study and is relatively well understood.

Management action research requires as its basic data inputs a variety of quantitative and qualitative measures related to technical and human levels of performance and satisfaction. The distinguishing feature is the fact that these measures serve directly to define the nature of management intervention which will be made in an attempt to modify the behaviour of the system in question. Specific examples of possible types of measures include measures of workflow, job satisfaction, the structure of an organisation, the interpersonal/intergroup relations defined by it, and a range of indicators of organisational performance. Such measures need to be gathered within the framework of a continuing, on the site, data collection process which will permit immediate analysis and the rapid identification of major organisational problems. In addition, the analysis must be designed to suggest the immediate interventions necessary to overcome such problems.

Operational research, of course, represents the most limited scope of the research methods, involving primarily the construction, validation, and optimisation of analytical/quantitative models describing a particular operational task within the organisation.

Information Output

Policy research aims to produce policy options and (in particular circumstances) prioritise recommendations.

Evaluation research results in two kinds of research output. An identification of facility/program strengths and weaknesses and an outline of the major factors which determine program success.

Management/tactical research findings can be classified as either exploratory or definitive. Exploratory findings present management with an in-depth description and interpretation of available information related to the decision situation. Such information can be provided relatively quickly and permits management to make a more informed decision concerning whether action can be taken in the light of available knowledge and real world competitive and time constraints. Should the collection of additional information be necessary and feasible, the exploratory research will have clearly specified these in-depth information needs. Definitive findings are the result of such in-depth research and should provide management with a clear understanding of the situation, followed by precise recommendation for actions to overcome the original problem or to take advantage of an opportunity.

Action research is designed to provide suggested courses of action that can be immediately implemented and the results of the implementation followed and studied. As such, the process is continuous and interactive. Types of action suggested by this type of research involve changes in the work environment to improve technical performance or human satisfaction, modification of the reward/punishment system related to performance, and changes in organisational structure designed to increase operating effectiveness.

Operational research provides management with precise answers to precise operational questions. These answers may take the form of explicit decision rules prescribing the required operational actions under all probable conditions. Alternatively, or in parallel, the research findings may be presented as precisely defined "management by exception" task performance measures indicating when management is required to step in and take corrective action. In brief such results consist of highly detailed instructions concerning "what to do, when to do it, how to do it" in relation to specific tasks within the organisation.

Table 6.1 attempts to summarise various research methods and data collection frameworks appropriate to various research categories. It is hoped that the proposed framework for relating major research approaches to three important dimensions of the process of tourism management has clarified to some extent the question as to the distinction among different categories of research methods and the type of decision situation to which each is most relevant. These distinctions among research and data collection methods should not, however, obscure an important common characteristic and goal of all management research: an ability and desire to provide systematic and objective information for executive decision making which is timely and relevant and which ultimately improves the effectiveness of the organisation.

TABLE 6.1

IMPLICATIONS OF THE CLASSIFICATION FRAMEWORK CONCERNING RESEARCH METHODS AND DATA COLLECTION FRAMEWORKS

Research Category	Nature of the Management Situation	Type of Information Data Required	Principal Data Collection Methodologies Instruments	Appropriate Methods and Techniques for Extracting Information from the Data	Research Output from a Management Perspective
Policy Research	Need to provide well defined but broad guidelines which serve to establish priorities to direct the organisation's activities	Macro data related to present values and anticipated trends of major economic, social, technical, and political factors bearing on the organisation's activities.	Longitudinal/ time series measures of major indicators; expert judgement consensus measures (e.g. the Delphi method); large scale system stimulation (e.g. econometric and industrial dynamics models)	Methods which focus on predicting future conditions and their implication for the organisation; establishing priorities and trade-offs among alternative policies	Identification of key dimensions of future organisational priorities; recommend nature of action along dimensions; priority levels for alternative actions/policies
Evaluation Research	Need to know the extent to which completed and continuing programs are performing as projected and to identify the major variables influencing the observed performance levels	Data related to the evaluation criteria chosen to represent the objective of a particular activity or program	Measures of program utilisation levels, of satisfaction levels, of the evolution of performance of evaluation criteria over time through panel methods	Methods for evaluating historical performance with respect to relatively ill-defined and often changing objectives and conditions	Identification of program strengths and weaknesses overall and within different user groups; understanding factors influencing program success, recommend improvements
Management Tactical Research	Need for in depth understanding of specific limited scope management problems; often problems in a particular functional area	Descriptive information for understanding of key factors in problem situation, permits in depth analysis of influential variables	Technical and factual data bearing directly on the problem; also, awareness, attitudes, opinions, effectiveness/ alternative actions, behaviour	Maximum extraction form secondary data sources; surveys; experimentation; observation; models	Position paper; recommend-ations

Action Research	Understand ongoing operations and programs, modification potential; monitoring for continuos improvement	Continuous performance information; behavioural data re interpersonal and intergroup relationships	Measures of organisation/ program performance; qualitative, quantitative	Identifying problems from performance measures; ongoing behaviour, performance modification	Changes in the work environment; modification of performance reward/ punishment; changes in organisational structure
Operational Research	Establish decision rules to reduce management involvement and increase operating efficiency	High developed, reliable data pertaining to the performance of a very limited well defined task	Measures indicating level and dispersion of variable describing task performance (e.g. through mechanical devices)	Construction of analytical, quantitative modes followed by attempts to validate and optimise the models	Decision rules prescribing required operational actions under all probable normal conditions; "management by exception" task performance measures indicating when management is required to take corrective action

Study Activity 5

1.   *What do you understand by the following terms?*

    (i)   *Policy research*

    (ii)   *Evaluation research*

    (iii)   *Management research*

    (iv)   *Action research*

    (v)   *Operational research*

2.   How might research methodologies and data needs differ between each of the aforementioned categories of research?

3.   What answers will the various types of research outlined provide?

THE RESEARCH PROCESS & THE PURPOSE OF RESEARCH

We have seen that research is a fundamental business tool that assists in the making of decisions. The main form of research in tourism is marketing research but there has also been an increase in tourism impacts research. Tourism research tends to be difficult to gather, analyse and use because of the complex nature of its subjects: people and their behaviour, impacts on the environment; social change as a result of tourism etc.

Not only is tourism research difficult to measure and predict but it also is not easy to generalise. Most studies done are customised to fit the characteristics of a specific area, problem, or opportunity. Nonetheless, research must be conducted to keep ahead of the competition. Those that know what the wants and needs of their customers are in a better position to offer the right product. Those that know what impacts are detrimental to an area are better prepared to avoid them.

PLANNING RESEARCH

In planning a research programme it is important to

1.   Ascertain what you know about the subject of research by creating a detailed profile.

2.   Identify what you need to know and why?

    Determine what you are looking for and the purpose for which it will be used. Identify what is absolutely necessary to achieve your goals and objectives. This will help to determine the allocation of funds and define a possible course of action.

3.   Establish research priorities. Here it is necessary to:

    Address the most important tourism objectives first.

    Collect information necessary to meet the highest priority objectives

    Decide the most efficient way to collect the information needed for decision-making.

KEY REQUIREMENTS FOR GOOD RESEARCH

The key requirements for good research can be summarised as follows:

Utility	Can the research information be used?
Timeliness	Will the research information be available by the time the decision has to be made?
Cost-Effectiveness	Will the financial benefits outweigh the costs?
Accuracy	Will the information be accurate?
Reliability	Will the information be reliable?

DOING RESEARCH

There are two basic types of research: basic or **fundamental** and **applied**. Basic research focuses on new problems or new approaches to old problems. There is a necessary level of uncertainty with basic research and therefore success cannot be guaranteed. However, even the failure of approaches or research methods can advance the body of tourism research and thus should be encouraged.

Applied research tends to focus on problems that have been explored before, using approaches that have been successful in the past. Applied research is an excellent way to test established methods and to contribute to the solution of the problem.

Research is also categorised by the type of information used in the analysis, as illustrated by Figure 6.2 Primary research uses original data collected specifically for a particular research project. Secondary research uses data collected by others for purposes other than the particular research project in question. It is common to employ both methods of research when analysing problems or opportunities.

Study Activity 6

Choose any <u>one</u> article from the Journal Tourism Management. Does it use a basic or applied research approach? Justify your conclusion by referring to specific elements of the text.

Study Activity 7

Provide an example of <u>one</u> piece of tourism research that draws upon primary data and one that uses largely secondary sources.

Figure 6.2   Basic Methods of Research

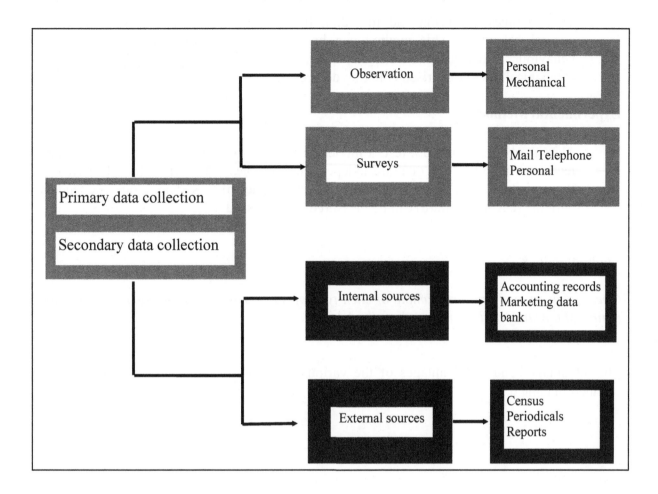

PRIMARY RESEARCH

Primary research implies that data is collected for the first time in response to a range of specific questions.

Here there are a number of applicable research methods. These include the use of:

- Surveys;
- Observation; and
- Experiments

Survey Methods

Three types of survey method are commonly employed:

Self Administered - questionnaires which people can fill out and return on the spot (e.g., suggestion boxes) or mail out questionnaires that are filled out and mailed in.

Telephone - questionnaires involving voice contact between an interviewer and a respondent.

Face to Face - questionnaires involving direct contact between the interviewer and the respondent.

Observational Method

This involves observing and recording the actions of a respondent or observing general behaviour. This method can be quite accurate because it studies actual behaviour rather than statements about behaviour. Observation also includes mechanical or computerised counting devices and registration methods.

Experimental Method

This involves setting up a test, a model, or situation to simulate the real world. The technique involves one or more independent variables which are allowed to change (e.g., visitor's opinions or reactions) and the impact of this change on a dependent variable (e.g., a brochure) can be measured and assessed.

Study Activity 8

Once again try and find an example of each type of approach in tourism research. Note the nature of the study and the research methodology employed.

The advantages and disadvantages of the various methods of primary data collection are outlined in table 6.2

TABLE 6.2

**THE ADVANTAGES AND DISADVANTAGES OF DATA COLLECTION
METHODS**

TYPE	ADVANTAGES	DISADVANTAGES
Experimentation	• good control over the situation being studied; therefore, the results are often given credibility	• often not applicable to many recreation situations except those of pure research
Physical Trace Evidence	• low cost • looks at intensity, density	• very crude measurement • outside influences can easily effect it (e.g., the number of garbage cans can reduce litter
Observation - Systematic and Participation	• valuable in small group studies • valuable for studying simple behaviour • good when useable to converse	• participation observation provides great opportunity for bias • accurate record keeping may be difficult • difficult to get detailed profile data • difficult to assess attitudes or opinions
Mechanical Observation	• generally low cost • little researcher bias on results	• device is fixed and cannot record outside its range • accuracy may be questioned e.g., children running back and forth through turnstile)
Face to Face interview	• can ask complex questions as interviewer is there to explain them • interpretation of questions can be clarified by the interviewer • interviewer can probe or ask for more detail in response • can build rapport between interviewer and subject by personal contact • best method for "open ended" questions (i.e., those that provide no choices for answers) • can record spontaneity with this method	• is expensive • can contact fewer people • interviewer may influence the respondent • interviews may not be consistent between different interviewers • time consuming • difficult to analyse if responses are detailed • may be awkward to ask questions on sensitive issues • may be difficult to arrange a meeting time

83

Telephone Interview	<ul><li>moderate cost</li><li>high response rate possible</li><li>quick</li><li>greater personal contact than with a questionnaire</li></ul>	<ul><li>interviewer may bias responses</li><li>must be short</li><li>cannot reach those with no phone</li><li>cannot ask questions with many alternates answers</li></ul>
Self-Administered Questionnaire	<ul><li>low cost</li><li>wide distribution is possible</li><li>good for obtaining factual information</li><li>less bias than other methods</li><li>easy to tabulate</li><li>uniformity of question presentation</li><li>can be fairly representative</li><li>people have time to put thought into completion</li><li>gives a sense of privacy and anonymity</li><li>can be completed when it is convenient for the respondent</li><li></li></ul>	<ul><li>response rate is often low</li><li>a slow process</li><li>questions cannot be too complex as they cannot be clarified</li><li>interpretation left up to the individual</li><li>impersonal</li><li>have no control over who completes the form</li><li>may be difficult to obtain currently mailing list</li></ul>
Public Meeting	<ul><li>facilitates information exchange</li><li>results of a course of action can be traced</li><li>agreement can be reached</li></ul>	<ul><li>usually not representative</li><li>often poorly attended</li><li>takes time and effort to publicise</li><li>special interest groups may "take over"</li><li>often used simply to give information and pacify groups (token gesture)</li></ul>

SECONDARY RESEARCH

The term secondary research refers to readily available information compiled by outside sources (e.g. OECD, EU or WTO). When properly analysed, secondary data may provide all the information needed to make effective decisions. All research should begin with a survey of the literature to determine what relevant studies have already been done, their results, their methods and any problems that they incur. This information can save a lot of time and effort in research direction, avoidance of errors, and in actual research if the necessary information is already documented. Some sources of secondary data are:

Government Studies (e.g. U.K.)

Visit Britain   Department of National Heritage
National Tourist Boards

Tourism Industry and Trade Publication (e.g. U.K.)

Inst. of Travel & Tourism,   Convention and Visitors Bureau
Tourism Society, ILAM
Chamber of Commerce

Magazines e.g. Imaginative Traveller
Brochures
Newsletters e.g. Business Tourism

Journals

Journal of Travel Research   Tourism and Hospitality Research
Annals of Tourism Research
Travel and Tourism Research Journal
Tourism Review
International Tourism Quarterly
Recreational Research Review
Tourism Management
Travel and Tourism Analyst

General Sources

Libraries
Regional and Local Government
Newspapers
Private data bases such as statistics/data from attractions/hospitality operations.

The foregoing discussion begs the question just how useful various methods of primary and secondary data collection can be in tourism research. Table 6.3 attempts to answer this question.

TABLE 7.3

RATINGS OF INFORMATION COLLECTION METHODS

Collection Method	Design			Usefulness			Cost			Administration		
	Easy	Med	Diff	Low	Med	High	Low	Med	High	Easy	Med	Diff
Primary Research												
○ Survey												
● Self Administered			X		X			X			X	
● Telephone			X		X				X			X
● Face to Face			X			X			X			X
○ Observing Behaviour		X			X				X			X
○ Counting Methods	X				X		X			X		
○ Registration Methods	X				X		X			X		
○ Suggestion Boxes	X			X			X			X		
○ Informal Surveys	X				X		X			X		
Secondary Research												
○ Desk Research Analysis	X					X	X			X		

Source: Adapted from: Alberta Tourism Community Tourism Marketing Guide

THE RESEARCH PROCESS

There is no one best way to conduct research and in fact different situations lend themselves to different approaches (Finn et al 2000). The process presented here is an outline of the steps that can be useful. Veal (2006) notes there is a degree of interaction and overlap between these steps because research is an exploratory process.

STEPS IN THE RESEARCH PROCESS

1. Identify the Problem and Establish Objectives

   Establish the problem
   Determine if problem exists in previous research

2. Determine Data Needs

   Ascertain what data is already available

3. Evaluate Possible Approaches

   Decide on research approach & methodology

4. Develop Research Proposal and Budget

   Devise sampling strategy
   Determine population to target
   Select the sample to represent population

5. Develop and Pre-test Research Instruments (e.g. questionnaire)

   Develop methods necessary to fulfil research aims
   Examine existing questions & methods
   Brief research staff
   Pilot questions/methods on a number of people
   Revise questions/methods given results of pre-test

6. Develop a Plan for Analysis

   Determine how data will be coded and/or grouped

7. Collect Data

   Establish time and place parameters for distribution and/or collection
   Determine how to increase response rate

8. Process and Analyse the Data

   Code and analyse data
   Summarise data in a meaningful way

9. Interpret and Report Results

   Interpret findings
   Present results using variety of methods, such as methods of central tendency and analytical statistics

Study Activity 9

(i)   *Distinguish between primary and secondary research.*

(ii)   *Outline five methods by which it might be possible to collect primary data.*

(iii)   *What are the major advantages of using secondary sources in tourism research?*

(iv)   *Outline the various steps in the research process.*

(v)   *Why is the collection of primary and secondary data important in tourism policy formulation?*

CONCLUSION

This chapter has attempted to identify and review the nature of information and research which is required to support effective policy development.

To this end the chapter has examined the role of research in tourism management decision-making; identified and classified research needs within any company/organisation; and discussed the research process. In the case of the latter, the key requirements of good research and how to undertake a research exercise were outlined.

Throughout the assumption is that policy decisions are based on the results of research and research activity. In this way research not only supports the policy making process, but also the more comprehensive and objective the research the better the policy decision.

APPLICATION

International Case Study: The development of a new International Conference and Convention Centre in London.

One of the major policy/ strategic decisions facing the city of London as a tourism destination is how best to expand/renovate its convention centre capabilities. While this issue has been studied on several occasions, there is still a certain level of discomfort within the industry on how best to proceed (Tourism Society May 2006).

Seek to prepare a research proposal in oral and written format that answers the following questions;

•   Does London truly need to upgrade its convention centre facilities, and if so why?

•   If a new/upgraded Centre is needed, what characteristics should it have?

        Here consider such variables as size, location, special facilities, number and types of meetings room. Consider how should such proposals be financed?

Your proposal should attempt to outline a systematic research process that mirrors the discussion in this chapter.

APPLICATION - A SAMPLE SOLUTION

THE LONDON INTERNATIONAL CONFERENCE & CONVENTION CENTRE - A DRAFT RESEARCH PROPOSAL

PURPOSE OF RESEARCH

To determine;

- If London truly needs upgraded convention centre facilities, and if so why?

- If a new/upgraded Centre is needed, what characteristics should it have? and how should it be financed?

RESEARCH AIMS

1. To identify major trends in the meetings and convention market that will likely affect any decision London might make to enhance its capability to serve this market.

2. To identify the size and nature of the segment of the meetings and convention market for which London might be competitive.

3. For this segment of the market, to identify those factors which are important in the choice of a site/location.

4. To determine current market perceptions of London as a meetings/convention site.

5. Based on current perceptions, to identify the changes that need to be made to London's existing meetings/convention facilities in order to be competitive.

METHODOLOGY

1. **To identify major trends in the meetings and convention market that will likely affect the decision London might make to enhance its capability to serve this market**

    - Review the literature in the field

    - Telephone interviews with selected industry leaders (meetings and convention planners)

    - Sample for interviews?

2. **To identify the size and nature of the segment of the meetings and convention market for which London might be competitive**

- Review secondary information sources that estimate the industry size (Visitor expenditure, number of attendees etc) distribution and seasonality of the following market segments

  - Conventions
  - Conferences
  - Corporate meetings
  - Association meetings
  - Trade shows
  - Consumer trade marts

3. **For each segment of the market, identify those factors which are important in the choice of a site/location. Such factors might include;**

- Location (city centre vs. other)
- Convention centre floor space
- Adjacent hotel rooms
- Flexibility of meeting rooms
- Convenient access
- Special technology
- Cost
- Local support
- Financial assistance
- Recreational possibilities

4. **To determine current market perceptions of London as a meeting/convention site;**

- How does each major market segment evaluate London on each of the choice factors that is important to it. This will in all likelihood require primary research (a survey of a sample of organisations in each market segment)

- which cities are viewed as being the most important alternatives to London for each major segment of the meetings and convention market (include as part of above survey).

5. **Based on current perceptions, identify the changes that need to be made to London's existing meetings/convention facilities in order to be competitive**

The following attributes need to be addressed.

Destination attributes - for reference only

- City as clean, safe, with access to pre/post activities
- Good air access: travel time, connections required, service by multiple carriers
- Hotel adequacy, size of hotels, number and quality of rooms and proximity to facility
- Price/value

- Quality convention and visitors organisation
- Local, involved organisations prepared to invite and host

Facility attributes - important

- Close proximity to large, quality hotels; walking distance of "10-15 minutes at most" (quality of walk is important - safe, interesting, weatherproof; physical connection to hotel desirable but not critical; adjacent hotels should have meeting rooms and banqueting facilities
- Downtown location, less of an issue for trade and consumer shows
- Safety of neighbourhood
- Good access to ground transportation and/or public transit
- Good traffic access - for materials handling and guest access

Facility attributes - less important

- Proximity to shopping (more important to convention than trade show delegates)
- Availability of parking (very important to trade and consumer show attendees)
- Location of airport to facility (within 45-60 minutes driving time)
- Connection to other public assembly facilities

Facility Design and layout - important *people* issues

- All services under one roof - no shuttles
- Design which minimises distances attendees must walk (i.e. from meeting rooms to exhibit space)
- Good function flow between meeting and breakout rooms and exhibit areas to facilitate access (and to encourage visitation of exhibits by delegates and to discourage leakage of delegates)
- Continuous exhibit space, ideally on one level; unencumbered (by pillars)
- Ample registration and crush area outside exhibit and ballroom areas (ability of space to handle more than one group registration at a time; wide vs. narrow
- Flexible exhibit hall and meeting room space (able to handle concurrent or multiple events and meeting rooms with different configurations
- Concourses of size/configuration to handle "wave" at adjournment
- Adequate office/business space for support workers
- Covered access outside building for taxis and pickup/drop-off

Facility Design and layout - important *materials* issues

- Two-way truck ramps to exhibit hall(s)
- Internal staging and off-loading areas for trucks (and internal holding areas)
- Separate vehicle exit/entrance points; vehicular access from more than one side of building

- Adequate truck parking close by facility
- Well-located service corridors and freight elevators to access exhibit and meeting rooms without disrupting ongoing activities

Facility - relatively important

- Functionality of *meeting* rooms - good blackout capability/ soundproofing/high ceilings for lighting, decor needs
- Functionality of *exhibit* areas - good power, recessed/piped water every 100/150ft/level flooring free of expansion joints/high ceilings/ good HVAC/Floor covering
- Technology needs - good basic infrastructure for audio/visual/ computer needs/ ext. data terminal hook-ups/plenty of telephone jacks throughout building/teleconference and satellite linkup abilities
- Expandability - room to expand with minimal disruption of support services (kitchen vehicular access, etc.)

Facility - relatively desirable

- Views from facility concourses, public areas (not meeting rooms)
- Natural light in building/above ground
- Aesthetically pleasing building (architecture and landscaping)
- Efficient security, particularly when simultaneous meetings are held
- Good access for the handicapped

FACILITY ANALYSIS

A Facility Analysis should be undertaken.

The accountancy group KPMG has performed a facility analysis and balance assessment for the purpose of establishing the proper facility size and configuration required to maximise London's potential in the meeting industry.

A comparison of London's peer cities provided the starting point for this analysis. Cities were selected based on population, location, market, climate and amenities. It is anticipated that some peer cities will be more successful than London in penetrating the meetings market while others will be less successful.

RECOMMENDED READING

Finn, M Elliott-White M Walton, M (2000) Tourism and Leisure Research Methods, Longman

Jennings, G (2001) Tourism Research, John Wiley and Sons

Ritchie, J R Brent & C R Goeldner (1994) Travel, Tourism and Hospitality Research, John Wiley and Sons Ltd., Chapters 7, 8 and 9

Veal, A.J. (2005) Research Methods for Leisure and Tourism: A Practical Guide, Longman

CHAPTER 7

Quantitative and Qualitative Research Strategies

CHAPTER OUTLINE

Research Techniques in Tourism Policy Formulation

Quantitative Techniques

- Nominal Group Technique (NGT)
- The Application of NGT to Tourism Policy and Planning
- Other Policy Situations
- The Strengths and Weaknesses of the Technique
- Comparison with other Research Methods
- Evaluation of Quantitative Techniques in Policy Formulation

Qualitative Techniques

What is Qualitative Research?

What Purpose Does Qualitative Research Serve?

The Limitations of Qualitative Research

Qualitative Research Techniques

- Focus Groups
- Interviews
- Panel Research
- General Household Surveys

What Makes Good Qualitative Research?

Qualitative Research in Action – The Banff-Bow Valley Study

CHAPTER OBJECTIVES

Having read this chapter and undertaken the various study activities you will be able to:

- Understand the importance of quantitative and qualitative research in making policy.

- Be able to suggest a range of different research techniques that could be used to collect data on which to base a policy decision

- Evaluate the strengths and weaknesses of these aforementioned techniques as a means of collecting data used in tourism policy-making.

RESEARCH TECHNIQUES IN TOURISM POLICY FORMULATION

1. QUANTITATIVE TECHNIQUES

It is not the intention of this text to dwell on all the various techniques that are used in conducting research. These are more than adequately explained in Veal (2005) Jennings (2001) and Finn et al (2000). Rather the chapter will focus on somewhat more peripheral techniques used in the process of policy making.

The chapter will argue that various approaches to research adopted in the process of policy-making go through cycles of rising or falling popularity or fashion. At the time of writing this text, qualitatitive rather than quantitative paradigms dominate with policies frequently being developed on the basis of an analysis of stakeholder attitudes and opinions

THE NOMINAL GROUP TECHNIQUE

The NGT procedure, as used for program planning, is normally implemented in six stages. Participants are first presented by the session moderator with an initial statement of the topic area to be discussed.. Top management of a corporation might be asked to indicate what directions future diversification would take, for example. Once it is clear that participants understand the issue, further discussion is halted.

Participants are then directed to reflect individuality on the topic and to record their personal responses on a worksheet containing a written statement of the issue being addressed. This period of individual reflection and recording of responses usually lasts from 5 to 20 minutes, depending on the complexity of the topic under discussion.

The group moderator subsequently asks a participant, chosen at random, to state one of the responses she or he has arrived at individually. This response is written in a concise yet complete manner on a large flipchart. At this point, the participant is allowed to explain his or her response briefly, so that its meaning is clear to other participants. This process is repeated in round-robin fashion until all participants have had a chance to express a response. Second and third rounds may follow, depending on the number of ideas identified by members. Participants are allowed, and even encouraged, to express additional ideas that have been stimulated by the remarks of others.

The next stage involved consolidation and review of the complete set of ideas. At this point, all flipchart sheets are posted so that all responses are visible. The moderator reviews the responses recorded on the flipcharts to eliminate duplications and to ensure that all responses are clearly understood by participants. Each response is then assigned an identifier code, such as a letter of the alphabet.

Participants are subsequently requested to establish the relative importance that should be accorded to each of the response ideas. This importance may reflect, for example, the desirability of a given idea for corporate diversification. Although various approaches may be employed to establish the importance of each response, a commonly used method is to instruct each individual first to select a certain number of responses (e.g. eight) that s/he considers to be most important. The participant then writes each of these responses on a 3 x 5 card, along with the alphabetic identifier, and is asked to rank the eight responses in terms of their relative order of importance.

The final stage is compilation of the results. In this stage, the ranking accorded to the various ideas by each participant are aggregated to provide a measure of overall importance. As per the Delphi technique, these results may be presented to participants, and a second round of ranking undertaken to permit individuals to adjust their judgements in the light of the earlier evaluations. However, this round is not essential unless the initial judgements were highly variable or unless the purpose is to achieve a reasonable level of group consensus.

To summarise, the NGT process is a systematic approach designed to provide two specific types of output: first it provides a list of ideas relevant to the topic in question; and second, the technique provides quantified individual and aggregate measures of the relative desirability of the ideas raised in the session.

AN APPLICATION OF NGT TO TOURISM POLICY AND PLANNING

In the early 1990s the private sector in the British Tourism industry got together under the auspices of Tourism 2000 in order to formulate a coherent statement of its views concerning the direction that tourism development should take in the country. While it was recognised that the size and diversity of the public sector would never permit the preparation of the type of policy statement that is possible within a government agency, Tourism 2000 saw the need to develop a consensus of its members' views, which would serve to focus the organisations efforts and prioritise its actions. It was with this in mind that Tourism 2000 undertook a three-phase programme designed to set out the views of the private sector concerning provincial tourism development and promotion. The contents of each phase were defined as follows:

- **Phase I**   Definition of priority issues and problems facing tourism in the province.

- **Phase II**   Identification of initiatives, actions, and programs to deal with priority issues and problems

- **Phase III**   Monitoring of recommendations concerning initiatives, actions, and programs for tourism development to ensure timely and effective implementation.

OTHER POLICY SITUATIONS

At least two other planning tasks lend themselves to the application of the nominal group technique. The first of these relates to *organisational goal setting*. In this context, the process serves first as a means of eliciting a set of statements defining the mission and the objectives of the organisation. In the case of a private sector tourism operator, these goals would normally relate to the overall direction of the firm and the specific achievements it hopes to realise within a specific time frame. For a public sector organisation, the process would normally involve attempting to specify the economic and social contributions it is hoped will be achieved through tourism development. In both cases, once the organisational goals have been defined, the NGT process provides a mechanism for determining the relative priority the top management wishes to accord to the various goal statements that have been proposed.

A further area of application relates to the *identification and evaluation of alternative courses of action* for resolving a management issue. In this situation, NGT can first be used to generate a range of possible solutions to the problem or opportunity facing a management team and then can be subsequently employed to rate the perceived effectiveness or desirability of the options generated.

In addition to being employed as an internal tool for organisational planning, NGT can be very effectively employed in *consumer research* as an alternative means of data collection. In this regard, NGT provides a methodology that falls between unstructured focus group techniques and structured survey methods. Examples of the kinds of consumer research that might be addressed by NGT would include:

- Studies to identify and establish the relative importance of factors that consumers view as critical in determining the quality of service in a hotel, a ski resort, or other tourism facility.

- Studies to identify and establish the relative importance of information sources used by consumers when choosing among alternative types of tour packages.

- Studies to identify the dimensions that are important in defining the images of different countries as travel destinations.

By extension, it is seen that NGT can be adapted for use in the study of most research questions in which individuals are required to generate ideas and, subsequently, to provide some rating of the ideas' relative desirability.

A second research application of NGT is an alternative to the Delphi technique (Linstone and Turoff 1975) when attempting to obtain *expert consensus* on a given research topic. While the Delphi method is effective when respondents are geographically dispersed, it is somewhat cumbersome and time-consuming unless it can be conducted in an electronic format. In contrast, in situations where experts can be physically brought together, NGT provides a very effective data collection approach. Examples of potential applications in this area include:

- Research to identify and determine the relative importance of factors influencing the choice of meeting and convention sites.

- Research to examine how wholesalers assess the attractiveness of proposals submitted by different travel destinations and suppliers when assembling their tour packages.

- Research to identify those regulations and laws that are most severely impacting on the success of private tourism operators.

Again, as in the case of consumer research, NGT is appropriate in situations where it is required to gather and structure information from a defined group of respondents who can be brought together for a limited period of time.

THE STRENGTHS AND WEAKNESSES OF THE TECHNIQUE

Several strengths can be identified. First, although a group method, NGT provides structured output that can be analysed at an individual level. The term *nominal group technique* is intended to suggest that the method is *nominally* viewed as group based although, for the most part, the activities and output focus on individual efforts. The early stages of the process provide respondents with the opportunity to hear the views of others as they are thinking through the topic under discussion - similar to other group methods. On the other hand, the final stages require respondents to sort and rank the items generated in earlier stages. Thus, the data output is more structured than is usual with group methods.

Second, the NGT process results in high respondent involvement and commitment. This commitment develops as respondents express their views to others in the group and realise that they are sharing in the identification of items to be evaluated. This advantage can be particularly useful when participants need time to think through their responses. This is not to imply that they are thinking up new ideas in a creative sense. Rather, when asked to recall behavioural experience, it is probable that respondents have had little experience identifying the various steps that were involved in the behaviour. In other words, although the behaviour of interest may be current or even habitual, the process of articulation requires time and commitment to recall the various components.

Third, the process of identifying and scoring problem themes, as developed in this application, makes it possible to study both intra- and intergroup differences.

The major disadvantages of NGT relates to sampling. Because participants have to agree to come to a central meeting location, attempts at probability sampling are met by a serious level of nonresponse, as discussed further in the following sections.

COMPARISONS WITH OTHER RESEARCH METHODS

Although NGT is not seen as a substitute for structured survey methods, it is useful to draw several contrasts. A summary of the major strengths of structured research methods would be: (1) ability to cover a large number and range of items, (2) use of probability sampling, and (3) structured output that facilitates analysis. The difficulties associated with these methods include: (1) problems inherent in establishing questions or items that are relevant to intended respondents, and (2) maintaining control of the interview setting. The former problem is handled by careful exploratory research and pre-testing. However, despite methodical preliminary efforts, most researchers have experienced studies in which some aspect of the research problem has been under-measured. The second problem mentioned, controlling the interview setting, is related to the use of a large number of interviewers. In a field situation, interviewers often feel a pressure to hurry the interview and, as a result, respondents are not encouraged to think out their answers. Further, as the questionnaire length increases, the interviewer has increasing difficulty maintaining respondent interest and commitment.

The strengths and weaknesses of NGT methods are almost the mirror image of those associated with survey methods. The advantage of probability sampling is not available with NGT. Although both methods provide structured output, the range of topics that can be covered is reduced with NGT. On the other hand, the problem of establishing items that are relevant to the intended respondents in enhanced. Furthermore, the control of the interview setting is simplified by the highly structured NGT process.

To restate an earlier comment, the intention is not to suggest NGT methods as a substitute for structured surveys. However, the added structure of NGT, not normally available in group methods, together with the judicious use of multiple quota-based groups, may provide an opportunity to go considerably beyond the usual exploratory research.

EVALUATION OF QUANTITATIVE TECHNIQUES IN POLICY FORMULATION

The quality of policy and planning activities is no better than the quality of information on which these activities are based. In turn, the quality of this information depends upon the use of methods of data collection that provide appropriate, reliable inputs that can be analysed and interpreted so as to provide meaningful insights and conclusions. This paper has attempted to familiarise the reader with one technique that has found to be extremely useful and that it is believed deserves wider recognition and use by those involved in tourism management

DISCUSSION QUESTIONS

1.   Outline the principles behind the nominal group technique.

2.   What are the major strengths of the technique?

3.   How can this technique be used in policy formulation and strategic planning?

Study Activity1

Go through several of the well know journals in tourism. Here Tourism Management and Annals of Tourism Research are particular good. Find three examples of where NGT was used in tourism policy-making

RESEARCH TECHNIQUES IN TOURISM POLICY FORMULATION

2. QUALITATIVE RESEARCH

WHAT IS QUALITATIVE RESEARCH?

Qualitative research is the foundation on which strong, reliable research programs are based. It is most often the first step in a tourism policy research program - the step designed to uncover motivations, reasons, impressions, perceptions, and ideas that relevant individuals have about a subject of interest. Unlike more quantitative methods of research, qualitative research involves talking in depth and detail with a few individuals. The goal is to develop extensive information from a few people.

With quantitative research, the goal is to develop important - but limited - information from each individual and to talk with a sizeable number of individuals in order to draw inferences about the population at large. The characteristics of qualitative research, on the other hand, include small samples, extensive information from each respondent, and a search for meaning, ideas, and relevant issues to quantify in later steps of the research program.

WHAT PURPOSE DOES QUALITATIVE RESEARCH SERVE?

Qualitative research can be used to address a number of different objectives namely:

- The development of hypotheses

- To identify a full range of issues, views and attitudes that need to be explored in the process of policy formulation.

- To suggest methods for quantitative inquiry

- To develop new product, service or marketing strategy ideas

- To provide an initial screening of new product, service or strategy ideas

- To learn how communications are received.

THE LIMITATIONS OF QUALITATIVE RESEARCH

The findings from a qualitative research effort must be regarded as informed hypotheses, not as proven facts. The samples that are used are quite small and usually selected in a purposive rather than a probability-sampling procedure. Thus, the inferences that are made based on qualitative research are normally subjected to evaluation using quantitative procedures at a subsequent time. Hypotheses, issues, ideas for new product/services, or communications strategies need to be confirmed on more reliable samples before major decisions are made.

In addition, qualitative findings may be limited by the skill, experience, and understanding of the individual gathering the information. Thus, the skill of a group-session moderator to draw out all participants to reduce domination by some members of the group, and to develop sufficient rapport to gain truthful information from participants must be assessed in judging the value of a group-session study. Additionally, when individual interviews are used in a qualitative research effort, the interviewers asking the questions and probing responses may also influence responses and perhaps bias the results. A number of interviewers each doing a small number of interviews helps to control for this potential bias.

QUALITATIVE RESEARCH TECHNIQUES

Two basic methods of data collection are used in qualitative research: the individual interview and the focused group discussion.

(i)   **Focus Group Discussion**

In a focused group discussion, eight to ten relevant individuals are gathered together to discuss a topic under the leadership of a trained moderator. One key benefit of this approach is the interaction among respondents. Each individual is free to argue, disagree, question, and discuss the issues with others in the room. Thus, the group session becomes most useful when exploring a broad range of attitudes and views, when searching for a variety of responses, and when interaction is a plus for the study.

Additionally, group sessions in most locations can be done in professional facilities with one-way mirrors and sound systems so that the discussion can be observed by others. So, if observation by one or members of the management or research team is desirable, focused group discussions could be suggested. Care must be taken, however, to ensure that hearing a few customers discuss a topic does not lead management to make premature decisions on the subject.

On the liability side, the major drawback to using groups in the qualitative research process is that despite the efforts of a trained moderator, some individuals may dominate the discussion, leaving open to question whether the views obtained are biased or prejudiced in any way because of the group dynamics or the group leader. Concern with biasing of this type is most important in studies designed to screen out product/services that offer limited opportunities for development. In cases where the goal is to develop a range of views or attitudes, the problem is not so serious. though it may mean that one or more groups have been less productive than should have been true.

Study Activity 2

Aim to set up a focus group with several of your peers. You decide on the topic for discussion. What problems did you experience in bringing together and moderating the group?

(ii)   **Individual Interviews**

Individual interviews are used most often in qualitative research when the interaction of a group is not desirable, when the goal of the research effort is to understand a process or an event in which each individual must talk at length about how he or she went about doing something. Individual interviews are particularly useful in travel research when the goal is to understand, for example, how travellers go about making a decision to take one vacation trip versus another. To gather that information, it is necessary to delve into each person's decision process at length - to learn where the ideas originated, what information was gathered, who was consulted, whose views were sought out, and, finally, what led the individual to make a choice for one opportunity and to reject the others.

Where this type of information is sought from each individual, the group process breaks down. It is reasonably boring and uninteresting for each participant in a group to sit and listen to the decision process through which another participant went. Interaction is of little importance in these types of studies, and, therefore, groups are replaced with a series of individual interviews.

On the limitation side, individual interviews require that a reasonably careful topic guide be written prior to the start of interviewing. Since a number of interviewers will conduct the interviews, the process has to be well defined prior to the start of interviewing.

Each interviewer uses the general questions posed and probes with his or her own additional questions to gather more meaning. Thus, with a number of interviewers, the probing questions may differ, and each may get slightly different information. In a qualitative study, such variations are often beneficial since they bring to light a broad range of views and insights.

In comparison with groups, it is much more difficult for interested marketers and researchers to observe such individual interviews, and these interviews can frequently be quite costly. Interviewers must be specifically trained to conduct these interviews, and that training cannot be amortised over too many interviews since each interviewer does only a small number.

(iii)   **Tourism Panels**

Consumer panels have played an important role in studies of consumer purchasing patterns, including such leisure interest trends as television viewing and dining out. Less well known are the numerous industry panels of dealers, agents, retailers, and various professionals that also are valuable sources of market trends and insights.

Although panels are usually viewed as a longitudinal survey technique, they do have important uses other than trend monitoring. Many new products arriving on the market, for example, have received extensive testing by panels. Because of their stand-by capability, panels also are valuable for assessing the social impacts of unforeseen events. Voter panels as well as panels of specialists have been used effectively for short-term predictions. Each of these uses has potential applications for travel and tourism research.

Panels for Trend Monitoring

Reliable facts and figures on trends in tourism are surprisingly scarce in light of the high values placed on such data by planners and investors. While available indicators such as park visits, passports issued, commercial lodging, vacation trips, airline travel, and gasoline consumption provide gross estimates of tourism trends, their value for planning purposes is limited. Questions of travel market shifts, interactivity substitutions, changing travel interests and frequencies, planned equipment purchases, and travel intentions reflect a more ideal level of detail for corporate planning. This kind of data, along with documented trends in tourism developments and profitability, could spell the difference between sound planning and superficial planning. Such trend data can best be generated by longitudinal studies of specific populations.

Longitudinal studies of tourists can be classified broadly as: (1) independent samples (resurveys) of a given population at two or more points in time, or (2) repeated measurements of the same sample (panels) over time. Both approaches have distinct applications for the study of travel and tourism depending on the specific research objectives . In general, resurveys are best for monitoring gross changes in large populations over extended time intervals; panels tend to be more commonly used for sensitive monitoring and in-depth studies of the factors (attitudes, interests, etc.) that may have contributed to those changes.

Most commonly, longitudinal studies take the form of periodic resurveys in which a new sample of the population is drawn for each survey. In the U.S.A. the national Boating Surveys (U.S Coast Guard), The National Hunting and Fishing Surveys (U.S. Fish and Wildlife Service), The National Camping Market Surveys (USDA Forest Service), and The National Outdoor Recreation Participation Surveys (U.S,. Department of the Interior) are federally sponsored resurveys conducted at approximately five-year intervals. A number of states, industries, and non-profit research centres also conduct periodic travel and tourism surveys. The U.S. Travel Data Centre, for example, conducts a telephone survey of 1,500 adults each month to gather information on travel behaviour. The Commerce Department's periodic Surveys of National Travel, Retail Trade, Purchase of Durables, and Consumer Expenditures all provide opportunities for analysis of tourism-related trends. While obviously better than the available indicators, population reserves are still basically descriptive and have a limited capability for explaining trends and shifts in leisure-related travel.

For longitudinal studies with greater explanatory capability, it is sometimes desirable to periodically re-contact the same sample of respondents. Panels are superior for providing in-depth answers to questions of why market shifts and trends are taking place. An eight-year-long travel-oriented panel study conducted by the USDA Forest Service to document trends in camping participation showed clear relationships between family life-cycle stages and styles of camping participation. The study also documented the impacts of crowding on camping participation and the impacts of crowding on camping frequencies and destinations.

Panels of tourist businesses are more common than panels of tourists and have provided useful indexes of changes in business volume and profitability. In the U.S., one of the longest such series (23 years) is the Economic Analysis of North American Ski Areas conducted by the University of Colorado's Graduate School of Business Administration. This survey uses essentially the same sample of respondents each year (Goeldner et al. 1992). A similar commercial campground industry survey that has been in operation since 1979 provides a biweekly occupancy index (National Campground Owners' Association 1981).

Panels for Test Marketing

The availability of existing consumer panels, whose primary purpose is to track changes in purchasing patterns or in television viewing, provides an ideal opportunity for the test marketing of new products. Pilot television shows are evaluated in just this way to determine their potential for development into a continuing series. Comparisons of competing household products are frequently made by panels of homeowners who receive unidentified product samples for blind testing. Such panels can require intensive researcher-client interaction, including lengthy interviews, diary records of expenditures and use of time, and even the installation of recording instrumentation in the home, such as television audiometers.

While most panels exist with the full knowledge of the panel members, it is also possible, in fact highly likely, that most people have served on informal test marketing panels without knowing it. Mailing lists of credit card holders or college alumni, for example, may be sent brochures offering "discount" rates for vacation tours. The response rates are analysed and, if favourable, the list becomes targeted for additional promotions - a de facto panel whose responses are purchases instead of opinions! In a similar fashion, buyers of chainsaws, garden tractors, television sets, guns, campers, snowmobiles, and so on, are often provided with a warranty containing a brief questionnaire that must be returned to the manufacturer for validation. The buyer gets his warranty and the sales department gets a mailing list, a purchaser profile, and a test-marketing panel.

The possibilities for establishing both formal and informal panels of travellers and tourists are clearly unlimited - every reservation, registration, and most equipment purchases and travel tickets can contribute to a potential master list for sampling promotional targeting and policy evaluation. The advantages of these informal panels are that they are already "in the market" and are inexpensive to establish. The disadvantage is that they can tell the researcher little about the market's potential size and distribution - critical facts for large-scale test marketing.

While the emphasis on panel research has been in the realm of long-term trend monitoring, the value of panels for short-term studies and experimental uses should not be over-looked: Entry and exit surveys at recreation areas or on cruise ships constitute a form of short-term panel ideally suited to matching visitor expectations and satisfactions. Short-term panels using diaries have been effective in studying seasonal changes in leisure behaviour. Club memberships, subscription lists, and visitor registration afford outstanding opportunities for experimental panels to test the effectiveness of different promotional strategies. In terms of available sampling frames, the opportunities for using short-term panels to assess consumer acceptance of new travel products and tour-promotion packages have too often gone unrecognised.

Panels are ideally suited for a true before-after experimental design and, therefore, are capable of generating some of the strongest cause-effect data available to the social scientist. Once a panel's levels of travel expenditures, travel behaviour, and travel attitudes have been determined, the panel can be subjected to stimuli in the form of promotional materials, price incentives, or new information, and then the panel's response can be determined. Sophisticated, split-sample designs can introduce the elements of control and of multivariate analysis. In this way, the images of various tourist destinations and travel modes can be determined and the effectiveness of a variety of measures to enhance those images can be assessed. The effectiveness of different tourism promotion might be assessed by first determining a base level of interest among the panel, distributing different brochures in a randomised block design, and subsequently re-contacting the panel to determine new interest levels, trip plans, or actual trips taken. Obviously, subjecting a panel to this type of experimental use may compromise the future use of that same panel for trend monitoring purposes, or even for further experiments.

Panels for future assessment

In the U.S. at least two major national surveys have used panels to estimate future consumer impacts on the economy: The Consumer Buying Expectations Survey (U.S. Bureau of the Census) and the Index of Consumer Sentiment (University of Michigan). Both surveys include two to four panel contacts per year for assessing expectations of major consumer purchases and consumer confidence in the economy. Planned purchases of cars, campers, and boats, along with probability estimates for taking vacation trips, are important indicators for the travel and tourism industries. To the extent that these expectations can be correlated with actual past consumer behaviour (via a trend-monitoring panel), their utility and reliability can be greatly extended.

In addition to panels of experts and panels of consumers, important future insights can be generated through the imaginative use of producer panels. Panels composed of equipment dealers, travel agents, park managers, airline stewardesses, and almost any group having constant contact with the travelling public are potential sources of information about tourists' unmet needs and dissatisfactions. It is safe to assume that there is a direct link between unmet needs and future market declines or shifts in market shares. The front line is an information source that is to obvious that it is all too often ignored by many market researchers and most managers!

(iv)   **Resident Surveys**

Travel industry policy planners must have timely information about changing travel markets in order not to be left behind in a rapidly growing industry. Some of this information is obtained from resident surveys.

Types of resident survey

There are three basic modes of resident or household survey: <u>mail</u>, <u>personal interview</u>, and <u>telephone interview</u>.

Mail surveys are the least expensive, allow the largest sample size within a given budget, avoid not-at-home bias, eliminate interview bias, permit longer questionnaires, and allow respondents to consider their answers carefully, perhaps checking with other household members to insure accurate information. On the other hand, mail surveys are the slowest of the three modes, often adding four weeks or more to the survey process. Moreover, they permit the least control over question completion, are subject to loss in the postal system, do not permit interviewer probing for detailed recall, permit too much respondent self-selection, and produce the lowest response rates. Low response rates in mail surveys are likely to produce nonresponse bias, as those who take part in the activity being studied are more likely to respond than those who do not.

Personal interviews have the virtues of shorter elapsed time between interview and processing relative to mail and of higher response rates either through repeated call-backs or by substituting similar households. The drawbacks of this mode are the high cost of interviewing, the difficulty of obtaining interviews in some areas due to crime or exclusivity, heavy training and field-supervision requirements, and poor interviewer supervision. In some cases, interviewers have been known to falsify interview records to achieve interview quotas.

Compared to personal interviews, telephone surveys are considerably less costly, produce results more quickly, provide for direct supervision of interviewers, and offer respondent anonymity that may improve response rates

Telephone surveys cannot be easily or accurately conducted among populations relatively inaccessible to the instrument. Compared to mail surveys, telephone interviews are more costly. However, they are superior in minimising lag between interview and processing, in maximising response rates, and in providing control over the interview.

Depending on the stage at which it is carried out, a resident survey can either serve as a benchmark for a later assessment of change or as a measurement of current perceptions. Different surveys can also be administered to local residents, since their involvement in the tourism industry and perceptions can vary.

(v)   **Delphi Analysis**

Formulating tourism policy often requires looking to the future for events that are likely to influence current decisions, as well as to evaluate future impacts of current decisions. If policy planners are to make informed decisions they must focus on the future and plan to meet it through current programme decisions.

When someone considers taking an important course of action, he or she usually solicits the advice of other people - often people who have some special knowledge of the proposed venture. These people will give their judgements of what will likely happen in response to the actions. In effect, these "consultants" make forecasts based on their own special insights and knowledge. Their counsel helps decision-makers to understand what may be encountered in the future and how the future can be dealt with.

The Delphi technique

The Delphi technique is a method used to systematically combine expert knowledge and opinion to arrive at an informed group consensus about the likely occurrence of future events. The technique derives its importance from the realisation that projections of future events, on which decisions must often be based, are formed largely through the insight of informed individuals, rather than through predictions derived from well-established theory.

The Delphi technique is based on the assumption that although the future is uncertain, its probabilities can be approximated by individuals who are able to make informed judgements about future contingencies. It is intended to provide a general perspective on the future rather than a sharp picture.

Instead of the traditional approach to achieve consensus of opinion through face-to-face discussion, the Delphi technique "...eliminates committee activity altogether, thus ... reducing the influence of certain psychological factors, such as specious persuasion, unwillingness to abandon publicly expressed opinions, and the bandwagon effect of majority opinion" (Helmer and Rescher 1960).

The Delphi technique encourages individual input by maintaining anonymity among those who take part in the process. Information relevant to the development of consensus is systematically fed back to participants by the Delphi Study director.

Several rounds of rethinking the problem, with information feedback provided after each round, usually results in a convergence of group opinion.

The Delphi technique replaces direct open debate with a series of questionnaires sent to a selected panel of experts. The general procedures used to conduct a Delphi investigation are outlined in Table 7.1. Successive questionnaire contain opinion-feedback summaries from previous panel responses. Feedback information includes summaries of reasons given by individuals for their responses about the probability, desirability, interaction, or impact of future events. This information serves to stimulate further thought about points that other panel members may have overlooked and allows them the opportunity to reconsider arguments they may have at first thought to be unimportant.

Delphi study results are summarised graphically to show the interquartile range of predictions. The median is most often used as the most probable year of occurrence because half the predictions fall above and half below that point. Independent events are often woven together to form an abstract concept of the future or to develop scenarios.

Study Activity 3

Take a look at Chris Ryan's paper on the use of the Delphi technique in tourism research. (Tourism Management 2005).

How has Ryan used the technique? What limitations in research methodology was he able to identify?

TABLE 7.1   Steps in Conducting a Delphi Study

Step	Procedure	
Identify relevant events.	Determine events from theoretical models, futures scenarios, or literature. Panel members may also suggest events.	
Prepare event statements.	Statements must be clear and precise.	
Select and establish panel of experts.	Select panellists from area of expertise suggested by the problem - expertise based on contributions to the literature and peer recognition.	
Mail Delphi questionnaire.	Questions asked of panel members.	Summary information sent to panel members.
Round 1 questionnaire	Assign probabilities and dates to events. Add events to list. Solicit information on ambiguous statements.	Edit event statements. Prepare response summary distribution showing individual responses.
Round 2 questionnaire	Ask individuals to re-evaluate their round-1 responses based on summary distributions. Ask panellists to provide reasons for changing or not changing their responses if they remain outside interquartile range.	Prepare interquartile response summaries for round-2 questionnaire. Edit reasons given by those outside interquartile range.
Round 3 questionnaire	Ask individuals to evaluate their round-2 responses based on summary information. Ask panellists to provide reasons for changing or not changing their responses if they remain outside interquartile range.	Prepare summaries of interquartile distribution of round-3 questionnaire responses. Edit reasons given by those outside interquartile range.
Round 4 questionnaire	Give individuals final chance to evaluate their round-3 responses based on summary information. Ask panellists to rate their expertise, evaluate desirability of each event, evaluate interactions between events, and evaluate social impact of each event.	
Other rounds	Questionnaire should continue until a consensus prediction begins to emerge.	
Data analysis	Prepare event summaries showing event distribution, probabilities, impacts, desirablities, and interactions. Use median prediction as most probable year of event occurrence. Prepare summaries of interquartile distributions. Prepare future scenarios.	

WHAT MAKES GOOD QUALITATIVE RESEARCH?

The criteria for successful qualitative research differ somewhat for focused group discussions and for individual interviews. The following sections point out some of the key elements in the assessment of each type of qualitative research.

1.   FOCUSED GROUP DISCUSSIONS

Several steps are key to having a successful focused group discussion:

First, all respondents must be *relevant* to the topic under discussion. It is critical that prospective participants be selected using a screening questionnaire that establishes their relevance to the topic; for example, should the study be designed to understand the full range of attitudes towards and impressions of a destination area, it is likely that all participants should have visited that area in the recent past.

To the extent possible, the screening questionnaire should be a *blind questionnaire* - that is, the respondent should not be able to detect just exactly who is sponsoring the study, what behaviour is being explored, and what attitudes will be sought. Naturally, it will be clear to respondents that the concern is with travel, but the specific destination or property should not be easily identifiable by the respondent during the screening process.

Additionally, there should be *exclusion of potentially biased people:* Anyone with special knowledge of or interest in the topic or the technique should be excluded. Those involved in advertising, market research, or any aspect of travel should not qualify as participants in a traveller group. Similarly, those who have participated in a group session or been interviewed individually in the past six months should be eliminated.

Second, to permit good information exchanges, good interaction and a lively discussion, all participants must feel comfortable presenting their views during the discussion. People are simply more comfortable discussing topics with "their own kind." Thus, one goal should be to do *separate groups* in most cases - younger apart from older people; white collar families apart from blue collar families; experienced international travellers apart from inexperienced ones; and so on. Such homogeneity is important in establishing psychological comfort for the respondents. This psychological comfort can be achieved with people of different demographic backgrounds if they have shared similar experiences recently that are relevant to the subject of interest to the researcher.

In designing a focused group discussion study, one group session with any population subgroup is seldom, if ever, sufficient. While a second session with the same subgroup may not be identical in content, if there are signs of consistency and commonality, researchers can confirm that neither is truly aberrant or deviant and, thus, be comfortable with inferences from the groups. In addition, should there be a need to conduct more than eight or ten groups (four or five different population groups) then it would appear that another, perhaps more quantitative research approach should be used. Upon completion of a group discussion study, the researcher still has only informed hypotheses, judgements, and ideas - not confirmed facts. Thus, spending time and dollars to conduct more than eight or ten focused groups and still not having facts on which to base a marketing decision is usually wasteful.

Third, the role of the *moderator* is critical in producing a good focused group discussion. The moderator is not only a director, but also a facilitator. He or she must develop rapport with the group participants, help them to relax and speak freely with each other, draw out the reluctant contributors, and keep natural leaders from dominating the conversation. The moderator's job is also to guide the discussion so that all important topics are covered and to probe and question (usually in a nonthreatening manner) to elicit the broadest range of information and views.

The moderator's topic guide should be thoroughly and completely worked out prior to the beginning of the session. The outline of questions should include the researcher's best thinking on the topics that must be addressed and the likely order in which they will emerge during the discussion.

The moderator, however, must be fully cognisant of the goals and objectives of the research, knowing which topic areas are most critical to cover in depth and which may be treated more lightly. In addition, the moderator must be sensitive to the emergence of unexpected information, ideas not anticipated at all by the research team, and must decide if and how to pursue those issues. One of the benefits of focused group research is that the moderator is free to gather new ideas, pursue new directions, and achieve new insights during the course of the session itself.

Fourth, the *physical comfort of respondents* in the group discussion should be of primary concern. Comfortable chairs and a well-ventilated room at the appropriate temperature are often as important in setting the tone of the session as are proper recruiting procedures and a good moderator. When appropriate, serving light refreshments also contributes to the development of the relaxed and informal atmosphere that is essential. Since most group discussions will last from one and a half to just over two hours, respondents need to be comfortable physically as well as psychologically.

Finally, the *analysis and interpretation* of the focused group sessions contribute importantly to the assessment of a successful study. The way in which the findings are approached and interpreted depends, of course, on the purpose for which the study was designed. Thus, it is not possible to suggest rules of interpretation that would apply to all analyses.

In reviewing the report on a focused group session study, the research/marketer should note whether the objectives have been addressed, whether the analysis covers the broad range of issues and ideas that emerged in the discussions, whether generalisations and conclusions are based soundly on the session input, and so on. The key assessment criteria should be: How useful are the results? How well do they guide and inform further steps in the research and development process?

2.   INDIVIDUAL INTERVIEWS

In designing a qualitative study that includes individual interviews, several steps are important to a successful study.

First, as with groups, the *participants need to be carefully selected* so as to be relevant to the problem under study; for example, should the issue be learning about the vacation decision process, then all participants should have taken the appropriate vacation, been involved in the decision process, and should have done so recently enough to remember the steps through which they went.

The screening questionnaire designed to identify these individuals should be carefully constructed to find only appropriate individuals and to eliminate those who could contribute only marginally to the study objectives. When only a few interviews will be conducted (15 to

30 is often an appropriate sample size), it is clearly critically important that each one contributes to the overall study goal.

Additionally, since studies in which qualitative research is accomplished through individual interviews usually seek to gain an understanding of behaviour or decision making from a variety of points of view, it is often important to include individuals with a variety of demographic characteristics to ensure that all population subgroups of importance are included in the qualitative research.

Second, the *development of the interview guide* is critically important. The careful assessment of all issues likely to arise in the conversation, ordering of topics into a likely sequence, and listing of possible probe questions are critical to the success of an individual-interview qualitative project.

Third, the *selection and thorough training of the interviewers* who will conduct the interviews form a crucial step in the individual-interview study. It is likely that the professional researcher who will ultimately analyse the responses to these interviews should conduct at least some of the interviews.

Interviewers being trained to conduct the interviews should observe the initial interview by professional researchers and be further trained in the goals and objectives of the project. They will need to ask additional questions and probes as they proceed through the interview as ideas emerge and are discussed.

Finally, *interpreting the results* of individual interviews is likely to be as varied as the purposes for which they were conducted. If the goal is to understand a decision process, then the results should include the variety of typologies that seem to occur in the process. If it is to understand motivations and reasons for particular behaviours, again, the interpretation should include the array of ideas gathered from the individuals who are included in the study.

Again, however, the interpretation and analysis are best judged on the basis of how useful the findings and recommendations are to the study as it progresses.

3.   TOURISM PANELS

The decision of whether to use a panel for travel and tourism research is a complex one. The panel approach must be appropriate to the objectives of the research and must be viewed in terms of organisational commitment. For trend-monitoring purposes, a simple listing of panel advantages and disadvantages is not very helpful to the researcher who must choose between a panel and periodic resurveys. The kind of detail desired in trend monitoring is far more important to the decision than the possibility that a panel, once established, might be useful for test marketing of for its stand-by potential.

Panels are often credited with being more economical than resurveys because sampling is only done once, and secondary contacts are often by mail. In fact, to be representative, the panel's composition must be constantly monitored, and procedures must be established for introducing replacements to the panel. Even if the follow-up contacts are by mail, the costs of panel maintenance may well offset that economic advantage. It is increasingly common for panel members to be paid for their services. Because of their continuing relationship, panel members often request follow-up information from the researcher. Unless one responds promptly to these requests, the panellists may lose interest and drop out.

Panels do provide a distinct advantage over other types of surveys in that they can tell the researcher a great deal about the non-respondent. As members drop out of the panel over time, they leave behind a useful file of their characteristics and pre-dropout purchasing/ participation patterns. And if budget restrictions require a mail survey rather than personal interviews, panels do tend to produce very high rates of mail response.

Panels are, of course, ideally suited to minimising the error in social surveys that result from faulty memory recall. And where the study objectives require detailed responses about quantities purchased, prices paid, dates, brands, expectations, and satisfactions, carefully designed panel procedures can serve to shorten the gap between the event and its reporting. Waves of questionnaires can be timed to follow seasonal fluctuations in travel, for example, rather than using one survey to cover a full year. Frequent participants, such as a panel of skiers, may be asked to record their activities in a specially prepared diary format. And the simple fact of being a panel member can make the subjects more alert to remembering the kinds of travel facts being asked of the panel.

Because panels are expected to provide detailed data, there is a concern that the panel may lose its representivity as it becomes sensitised to the objectives of the survey. Panellists may assume that their price reactions might help to lower prices. They may fine-tune their comparisons, becoming far more discriminating than normal, as their awareness and analytic abilities are tested. Panels of hotel owners may over-report their occupancy, and panels of restaurants may over-report meals served if they assume that the data might be interpreted as a gain in their market share. In fact, under-reporting, by consumer panels at least, is more of a problem than over-reporting. No matter how carefully the researcher designs his study, humans forget. In general, the bias from under-reporting due to forgetfulness is a constant and will have little impact on trend findings.

Because panels are considered sensitive social-measurement instruments, undetected errors can have serious consequences. So it is essential to undertake panel research only with a strong organisational commitment to the method to ensure awareness of the many potential error sources. By understanding the potential problems of panels, the researcher may be able to compensate for them, rather than discard the method. Concern relative to sensitisation of the subjects, for example, can be countered by a panel design that includes "controls" of different question wording and small-sample validity checks. Any survey contact produces a degree of sensitisation to the study objectives and may generate bias due to the respondent trying to please the researcher. As a suspected limitation of panels, sensitisation to the study objectives is probably exaggerated. In the case of the Forest Service camper panel, increasingly large numbers of campers were reporting that they were dissatisfied with conditions and planned to drop out of the market. Sensitisation was suspected; however, in comparing panel responses with those of a national market survey conducted during the eight year of the panel's existence, there were no significant differences in camper attitudes or participation patterns between panel members and non-members.

If sensitisation is the most overrated source of bias in panel studies, selective dropout is probably the most underrated. Panel mortality is often related to the factors under study. Camper-panel members would sometimes report that they had lost interest in camping and would no longer be responding. In assuming that their contribution to the panel was now unimportant, they seriously compromised the panel's potentially most significant findings regarding the nature and duration of market dropout. Similarly, those panellists who are most interested and involved are also more likely to be panel losses simply because they may be too busy to participate. In a panel of travellers, these may be the most important and most difficult panel members to retain.

While incentives and compensation may help to avoid potential panel losses, they are likely to do so not because of value received but because that value convinces them that their contribution is important. Stressing that importance, for example with telephone follow-ups to non-respondents, is probably the single most important guideline for panel maintenance.

Panels are clearly useful devices for travel and tourism policy research, both for long-term trend monitoring and short-term experimental testing. Long-term panels require considerable maintenance effort on the part of the researcher and are subject to a variety of sources of error from selective mortality, non-response, panel conditioning, initial selection bias, and underreporting. The potential effects of these errors on the survey results must be carefully considered in deciding whether to use panels or population resurveys. Despite the problems associated with them, panels are an effective and efficient way of developing indicators of change. There are many instances where consistency of bias is a reasonable trade-off for representivity, particularly when complete sampling frames are non-existent, making representivity an impossible objective.

4. RESIDENT SURVEYS

The problems of conducting resident surveys are well documented (see Veal 2005). Frequently identified problems are those of:

- Achieving a critical mass and valid sample size.
- The need for a representative sample
- Non-response
- Cost
- Interviewer bias
- Survey bias
- Complexity of administration
- Problems of recall and recall bias
- Duplicity and reliability of information

5. DELPHI ANALYSIS

The Delphi technique has been subjected to much criticism. Identification of panel experts and evaluation of their expertise present problems. Experts are usually busy people, and it is difficult to get them to serve on a Delphi panel for an extended period of time. Panel attrition can be severe. The effect of dropout has not been evaluated.

The Delphi study director can have a strong effect on study results. The events he or she chooses to include in the study and the way in which event statements are phrased can easily lead to misinterpretation. The study director can also influence results by editing panel response-feedback information.

The Delphi technique has been criticised because it usually treats events as independent of one another. It does not provide a way to evaluate the interaction between events. As well, an event's probability of occurrence depends largely on the general perspective assumed by panel members when they make their evaluations. If panel members do not share common perspectives, resulting predictions of events will be based on different criteria.

The Delphi technique has not been extensively tested in predicting events other than those directly related to technology. It has been shown to be most accurate in predicting technological events related to space and medical developments and in forecasting political alliances. The technique has had limited application for predicting events that involve human interaction.

Although based on many restrictive assumptions, the Delphi technique is useful where decisions have to be made quickly with limited knowledge. Indeed, in such situations, there may be no alternative. The need to make decisions today to meet tomorrow's leisure needs provides an example. It is easy for professionals in recreation to get tied up with everyday problems. Seldom can they see beyond next year's operating budget. But, if changing leisure needs are to be met, they must take a longer look into the future. The Delphi technique can help focus their thinking.

ASSESSING QUALITATIVE RESEARCH

The following series of questions may be used by a travel researcher/marketer is assessing the quality and effectiveness of qualitative research conducted. For the most part, the questions can be used for studies employing either focused group sessions or individual interviews.

- Are the objectives for the qualitative research clearly stated, appropriate for the techniques used, and targeted towards the marketing/research needs of the study?

- Is the number of groups and/or interviews appropriate for the problem? Are the population segments under study carefully delineated?

- Is the screening questionnaire tightly designed to eliminate all who will not be relevant to the project and who might create bias?

- Does the moderator's guide/interviewer's guide show clear and careful thinking about the issues to be explored and the logical flow of questioning?

- Is each group session conducted in facilities and with accoutrements that will generate both physical and psychological comfort for the respondents?

- Is the moderator/interviewer well versed in the goals and objectives of the study? Is he or she well trained and experienced in the professional skills required?

- Are the respondents comfortable with and able to talk with each other, and is the moderator without pretence?

- Are the topics of interest covered in sufficient depth and detail in each session/interview?

- Do the analysis and report reflect the full range of views expressed and generalise to the level of meaningful conclusions for further steps in the research effort or the marketing strategy development?

- Are all elements of the qualitative research effort handled in a professional manner?

If travel researcher/marketer can answer these questions in the affirmative, the qualitative research study should have contributed importantly to the solution of policy research and marketing problems.

QUALITATIVE RESEARCH IN ACTION

The Banff-Bow Valley Study

The Banff-Bow Valley Study was commissioned by the Federal Government of Canada in 1994. It took two years to complete.

Its purpose was to undertake a comprehensive analysis of the Bow Valley Watershed in Banff National Park (possibly the icon of Canadian tourism) The study sought to provide a baseline for understanding the implications of existing and future development and human use, and the impact of such on heritage resources. The study integrated environmental, social and economic considerations in order to develop management and land use strategies that were sustainable and met the objectives of the Canadian National Parks Act.

While the study made a number of far reaching policy statements, it was also notable for the way in which these policy initiatives were compiled, for the whole policy formulation process was based on consensus politics.

In the case of Banff-Bow Valley this involved extensive public consultation including questionnaires designed to solicit the opinion of people with an interest in the study area (vis residents, businesses and tourist organisations) and the use of the following techniques.

- Public meetings throughout the length and breadth of the country.

- Public debate via newsletters, community television, workshops, presentations and the Internet.

- Sectoral (or stakeholder) meetings where decision-makers were invited to attend.

- A storefront office was opened in downtown Calgary (the nearest large city) where the public could not only learn about the study but also discuss concerns, provide comments or review material.

- The establishment of a round table (or policy forum) chaired by an impartial mediator.

The Banff-Bow Valley Round Table was a broadly representative, highly participatory negotiation process and the primary mechanism for public participation in the identification of policies and the resolution of issues. From the outset it was the intention of the Round Table to break away from a pattern of confrontation of opposite views, to a common vision of the future. This represented a shift from consulting the public, to asking them to share the responsibility for making decisions about their National Parks.

The development of the Round Table was a first for National Parks Policy Planning in Canada. For the first time diverse and sometimes opposing interests in the valley sat around the same table and listened to each others concerns. It lead to an improved awareness of the issues and a better working relationship among various stakeholder groups.

In total fourteen stakeholder groups were invited to submit a representative (or Chair) to sit on the round Table (see figure 7.1). Some groups and businesses were not well represented. Others chose not to become involved. However, in the end, many people took the time to overcome the obstacles and find a common approach for managing the Banff-Bow Valley.

Figure 7.1   The Banff-Bow Valley Round Table

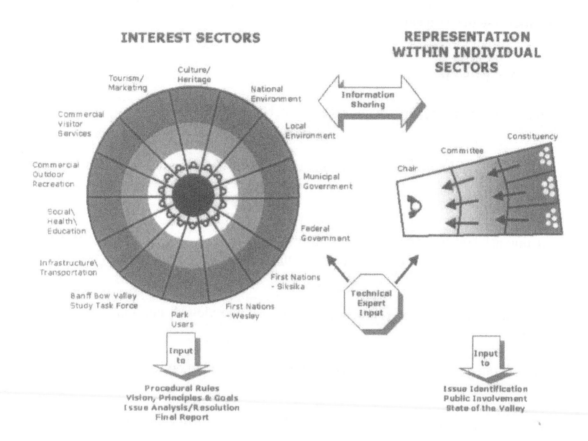

Participants in the Banff-Bow Valley policy planning process discovered that even if they were on separate paths, they headed towards a common goal or policy objective - a healthy environment for the Bow Valley in which a vibrant economic, social and cultural life was maintained. To this day this approach to consensus policy-making remains unique in Canada's National Parks for it provides an alternative model for policy formulation in sensitive tourist areas.

CONCLUSION

This chapter has considered how various quantitative and qualitative techniques underpin the process of data gathering and hence policy formulation.

It has been shown that in the current climate the trend is towards qualitative research. This in-turn has posed certain unique problems and opportunities for policy makers.

Throughout this chapter various case studies have been used to illustrate the relationship between policy-making and data gathering. This has culminated in a study drawn from the National Parks system of Canada.

DISCUSSION QUESTIONS

1.   What is meant by the term qualitative research?

2.   How might qualitative research techniques be used in the process of tourism policy formulation?

3.   Distinguish between (i)   Focus groups
                            (ii)   Individual interviews

4.   What makes for good focus group and individual interview discussion?

5.   Suggest three ways in which tourism panels can be used in policy research.

6.   What are the major advantages and disadvantages of using this technique in policy research?

7.   How might panels become "sensitised" to the objectives of policy research?

8.   What can be done to overcome this problem?

9.   Account for the phenomena of "panel mortality". What can be done to negate this issue?

10.   Outline the philosophy behind the Delphi Technique

11.   How might such a survey technique be implemented?

12.   What are the principal limitations of any Delphi study?

CHAPTER 8

Monitoring and Evaluating Tourism Policy

CHAPTER OUTLINE

Introduction

Monitoring and evaluation: key concepts and definitions.

The importance of monitoring and evaluation in tourism policy.

The politics of tourism policy: implications for monitoring and evaluation.

Conclusion

CHAPTER OBJECTIVES

Having read this chapter and undertaken the necessary study activities you should understand:

- The need for a systematic evaluation of any tourism policy.

- What is meant by the term 'policy evaluation' and what this entails.

- How, using the Graycar Model, it is possible to evaluate any tourism policy initiative

- What are the internal (organisational) and external factors that influence tourism policy evaluation.

- How policy evaluation can be seen as a political process.

Study Activity 1

Choose a tourism policy. Suggest some ways by which it might be possible to evaluate such a policy?

Clearly this is not an easy question to answer. Now read on ....

INTRODUCTION

> "evaluation is inherently political, and the acceptance of evaluation requires a 'community of men who share values' ... the requirements that must be met and the sacrifices made for an organisation to indulge in evaluative activity are so severe that they are rarely met."
>
> (Jenkins 1978: 228)

The systematic evaluation of tourism policy is a sadly neglected aspect of tourism planning, management and development. Given the dynamic nature of tourism, it has become increasingly critical for tourism policies to be monitored and evaluated. Policies are constantly changing in response to political, economic and social forces. Because of this, policies can become ad-hoc or incremental and lack appropriate goals and specific well-targeted objectives.

This chapter advocates the need for monitoring and evaluation of <u>all</u> tourism policies. In doing so, it examines key definitions and concepts, outlines the importance of monitoring and evaluation, presents a model for tourism policy evaluation and discusses some of the problems confronted in evaluating tourism policy. The chapter does not provide a discussion of evaluation techniques such as cost-benefit analysis or cost-accounting. Readers are referred to the recommended reading for references concerning those techniques.

MONITORING AND EVALUATION: KEY CONCEPTS AND DEFINITIONS

The literature on 'evaluation' is extensive, but there is no widely accepted definition of 'evaluation'. Thus, evaluative studies vary greatly in their comprehensiveness, methodologies and analysis of data. Dye (1992), for example, provides an interesting and detailed discussion of policy evaluation, but his work is somewhat limited. According the Dye (1992: 354), 'Policy evaluation is learning about *the consequences of policy'*.

'The word 'evaluation' needs careful definition. To most lay observers, it conveys a connotation of economic criteria ... But essentially, evaluation consists of *any process which seeks to order preferences'*. (Hall 1982: 288). Hall's definition of evaluation is insightful for two principal reasons. First, many other definitions of evaluation confine evaluation to the 'what happened after the policy was implemented' phase (e.g. Dye 1992). There is no reason as to why evaluation cannot be undertaken before a policy is put into effect or implemented. For example, it would seem to make good sense to include an objective whereby responses to policy *proposals* are evaluated. 'Because errors are to be expected projects should be planned to facilitate early detection and correction' (Hollick 1993: 125). Second, Hall's (1982) definition acknowledges that 'evaluation is not simply concerned with carrying out technically correct evaluations; it has to be concerned with how evaluation results are consumed and utilised' (Hogwood and Gunn 1984: 220). Tourism policy evaluation should therefore be concerned with who requested the evaluation, why the evaluation was requested, the estimation, assessment or appraisal of policy, including its development, content, implementation and effects, and the manner in which that evaluation will be consumed and utilised. Evaluation of policy must consider *why* who got what and where, and the outcomes and impacts of policy. That said, goals and objectives may be ambiguous or covert and therefore difficult to detect. This in itself means policy evaluation must go beyond simply measuring outcomes and impacts with respect to goals and objectives.

Tourism policy evaluation is an activity which is designed to collect, analyse and interpret information concerning the need for policy and the formulation, implementation, outcomes and impact of policies. Evaluations are undertaken for administrative, managerial and political purposes, for planning and policy development, and to meet fiscal accountability.

Rossi (1979) lists eight reasons why it is necessary to evaluate tourism policy.

- To assess the degree of need for intervention (by a government or organisation)

- To enlighten, clarify and improve policy.

- To provide conceptual and operational assistance to decision-makers.

- To specify outcomes and impacts.

- To assess or measure the efficiency and cost effectiveness of tourism policies in financial, human and capital resource terms.

- To provide an element of accountability.

- For symbolic reasons (to demonstrate that something is being done).

- For political reasons.

From the above discussion it should be clear that meaningful tourism policy evaluation requires:

- Some statement as to what the policy is expected to achieve.

- The continuous monitoring of decisions and actions throughout the process of policy formulation and implementation.

- The recording of impact (or consequences) of policy initiatives.

The constant monitoring of the tourism policy process alerts policy-makers to situations in which individuals carry out different activities from those envisaged or perhaps when policies fail to achieve the intended objectives.

Study Activity 2

Why might tourism policies fail to meet their intended objectives?

119

Policy failure or success could be the result of various aspects of policy design (e.g. ambiguous statements of objectives and intent), policy implementation (e.g. bureaucratic discretion or uncontrollable global forces), or from unforeseen forces (e.g. economic, political and social) creating changes in public need.

Evaluating tourism policies can prove difficult because:

(i)   It is not always clear what should be evaluated
(ii)   How policies should be evaluated and when
(iii)   Many policies are extensive
(iv)   The effects of policies may be difficult to detect.

Comprehensive policy evaluation is rare probably because it is expensive to conduct and because bureaucrats and decision-makers tend to focus more on day-to-day decisions than strategic planning. Truly comprehensive evaluation requires

*   Assessing and specifying the degree of need for policy and action
*   Monitoring the policy process
*   Specifying policy outcomes and impacts
*   Raising questions regarding the efficiency of tourism policy and its opportunity costs.

In reality most evaluation research is non-comprehensive (for reasons of expense) and confines itself to general statements about continuing, discontinuing, adopting or rejecting policies or improving specific aspects of policy performance.

By way of an example, listed below are some of the techniques that Tourism Canada uses to evaluate T C special events.

General techniques for the evaluation and control of events

Technique

1.   Each committee records all the major problems encountered, the solutions reached and a subsequent evaluation of the solution.

2.   Copies of all forms and formal letters such as fund-raising letters and registration forms should be filed.

3.   Copies of all publicity pieces produced such as tickets, booklets and fliers should be filed.

4.   All mailing lists should be filed.

5.   Audited financial statements with a comparison to budgets should be reported and the reasons for being over or under the budget stated.

6.   Attendance figures need to be reported including where the audience came from, what they liked, and how they heard about the event.

7.   Figures on local commercial activity during the event such as traffic counts, petrol station sales, hotel/motel occupancy rates, restaurant sales, and general merchants'

sales, are most useful for giving the festival economic credibility in a particular locale.

8.   An overall evaluation of the event by the executive committee in terms of its financial success, acceptability of individual events, and the success of individual publicity and promotion strategies is invaluable for the planning and management of any future event.

Study Activity 3

Study Tourism Canada's general techniques for the evaluation of events. Do you regard these criteria as comprehensive or non-comprehensive? Would you add anything else to the list? If so, What?.

THE IMPORTANCE OF MONITORING AND EVALUATION IN TOURISM POLICY

Much attention has been directed to policy implementation - what happens after policies are formulated (legislation passed or directives issued) - since the early 1970s. Pressman and Wildavsky's (1973) publication entitled *Implementation* is a classic text which sparked considerable academic and applied interest. Their subtitle was in itself revealing. *How Great Expectations in Washington are Dashed in Oakland; or, Why it's Amazing that Federal Programs Work at All, This Being the Saga of the Economic Development Administration as Told by Two Sympathetic Observers Who Seek to Build Morals on a Foundation of ruined Hopes.* The growth in attention given to studies of policy implementation in the last two decades has, in part, also led to an increase in interest in policy evaluation. If we accept Lindblom's (1980: 64) notion that 'Most, perhaps all, administrative acts make or change policy in the process of trying to implement it' then this observation in itself justifies the need for monitoring and evaluation.

Any attempt at evaluating tourism policies will be affected by

•   The clarity and specifics of policy aims and objectives.

•   Prevailing organisational priorities

•   Organisational change

•   Demographic and population trends

•   Changes in industry expectations and needs

•   Interest group reactions (acceptance or opposition)

•   Influences from community leaders, the moss media and business

Anderson (1984) suggests what is needed is an evaluation model that systematically evaluates cause and effect relationships and measures the impact of policy. Such evaluation models have, to date, been lacking due to uncertainty as who should evaluate, and how and when to evaluate.

Certain models have, nevertheless, been advanced (Chadwick 1971, Graycar 1983). In Graycar's policy evaluation model, four issues are seen to be paramount: conceptual issues, measurement issues, operational issues and political issues.

An evaluation of <u>conceptual issues</u> requires the evaluator to investigate (within limited guidelines) an existing policy. S/he may be required to:

- formulate an alternative policy; or

- determine policy guidelines to improve policy

To this end this might require

- problem identification

- the specification of a new set of objectives

- the analysis of weaknesses in the existing policy statement

- an examination of alternative policy scenarios

- on-going (formative) and summative monitoring of the process of policy formation and the impact of policy directives.

- Some demonstration as to the effectiveness of implementation strategies.

An evaluation of <u>measurement issues</u> requires the evaluator to determine the degree of emphasis to be given to hard (quantitative) or soft (qualitative) data. Neither of these data sources is mutually exclusive.

According to Carter and Wharf there are three main areas of evaluation research.

- Monitoring policy by means of audits (e.g. financial or administrative) and time and motion studies.

- Evaluating the social impact of policy by means of experimental research, surveys and case studies.

- Evaluating the costs and cost effectiveness of policy by cost accounting, cost-benefit analysis, programme planning and budgeting systems.

Evaluating the <u>operational issues</u> of any tourism policy requires:

- the evaluator to assess his or her relationship to all actors either within or outside the organisation. e.g. sponsors, planners, field workers, support workers, recipients etc. Policy, by its very nature can be threatening and potentially confrontational. Policy evaluation therefore requires that conflict situations are identified and resolved.

Other operational issues that need to be evaluated are:

- the constraints of time and money in influencing the process of policy formulation and implementation
- the effect of organisational constraints on policy development, and
- the influence of inter organisational relations in allowing decision-makers access to relevant information and individuals.

Policy evaluations are <u>political</u>, and 'Political problems are at the centre of any evaluation, because the decisions to be made on the basis of the evaluation (and indeed during the evaluation) are such that they fit into the political arena' (Graycar 1983: 172).

A skilled evaluator will take into account the political aims underlying the policy and analyse the extent to which the political system affects evaluation, and how the findings might be interpreted by Those with a vested interest, and with the power to implement or brush aside those findings.

Typically an evaluator will raise such questions as:

- Who is evaluating the policy and why is the policy being evaluated?

- What are the values, interests and expectations of the evaluator?

- If the study is not an independent one, who is underwriting the evaluation, and what are their values, interests and expectations?

- What are the potential outcomes of the evaluation in terms of resource allocations, policy maintenance or termination, and, ultimately, agency activity?

An outline of the Graycar model is provided in Figure 8.1. In studying this model it is important to remember that none of the four issues are studied in isolation. A comprehensive evaluation of tourism policy requires all four issues (conceptual, operational, political and measurement) to be addressed.

THE POLITICS OF TOURISM POLICY: IMPLICATIONS FOR MONITORING AND EVALUATION

> A positive advantage of evaluation would be to depoliticise a situation, to provide a cold rational appraisal of policy alternatives or policies *per se* outside the steam heat of emotion and ideology. Sadly, this is very much a false hope, a product of technocracy and scientism pushed forward by those who hanker after a managerial outlook and who fail to appreciate that there is really no such thing as an apolitical arena.
>
> (Jenkins 1978: 228)

It is because tourism policies are often long term; small scale low key and incremental; involve opportunity costs; and maybe influenced by a wide range of exogenous factors, that the impacts of such policies may be difficult to assess. There is also a real possibility that many tourism policies will be deemed to have failed if they are assessed simply in terms of their primary objectives, yet they may have generated positive benefits overall.

Policy evaluation should occur throughout the policy process. Policy evaluation may be inexpensive and involve as little as individuals reading documents and thinking about policy implementation and outcomes. At another extreme, it may also be very expensive and comprehensive involving an internal, external or combination of consulting teams. Policy evaluation is therefore concerned with trying to determine the process and impact of policy in real-life political conditions.

The monitoring and evaluation of tourism policies are not neutral. Above all other considerations, they are ultimately political tasks. Tourism policy objectives may be vague (and quite deliberately so), and the intended outcomes may not be explicit. Monitoring is much more than information collection and dissemination. According to Hogwood and Gunn (1984:221), monitoring

> requires decisions about what action will be taken if performance deviated unduly from what is desired. Thus monitoring is about control and the exercise of power. Those involved in programme delivery will be (and if they are not they should be!) aware of this, and this may affect how information about programme delivery is passed up to superiors. For managerial and political reasons, organisations may be unwilling to take the action which the monitoring information would otherwise indicate.

Figure 8.1   Graycar's Model for Evaluating Tourism Policy

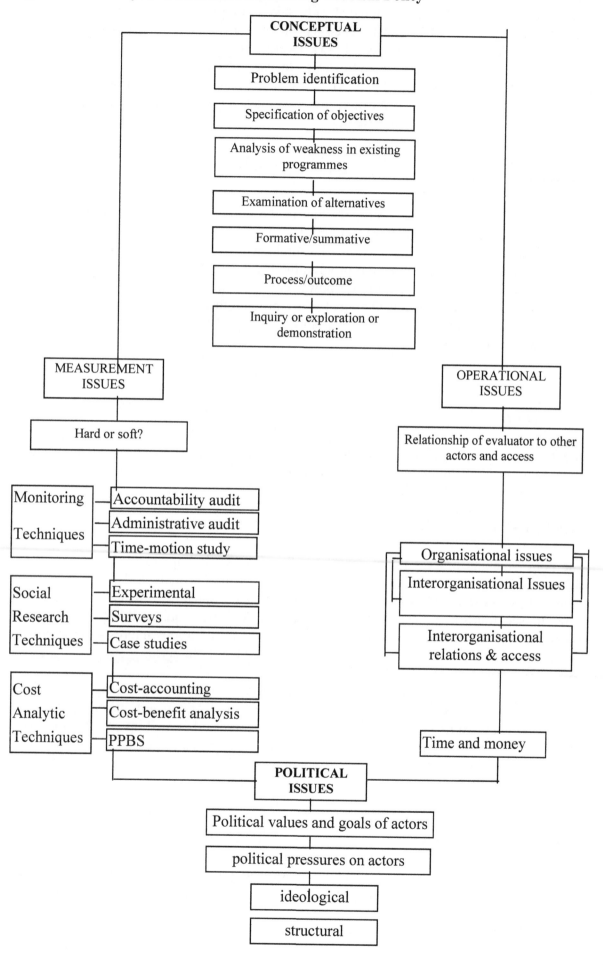

Policy-makers may use monitoring and evaluation to delay decisions and action; to justify and legitimate decisions and actions already taken; to pass the buck; to vindicate the programme in the eyes of its constituents, its funders, or the public; or to satisfy specified conditions (Weiss 1973), in Graycar 1983). Evaluations may thus be 'motivated by self service as well as public service, by a desire to use analysis as ammunition for partisan political purposes' (Anderson 1984: 135). As such, evaluations may even be undertaken to do little more than allay the fears of a few key interests, to defuse situations, to appear efficient, or to delay the political system.

Those who undertake evaluations of tourism policy would do well to recount Graycar's (1983) statement that:

> It cannot be stressed too strongly that in the initial conceptualisation of the evaluation, one must identify programme aims in terms of the politics of the actors, with thoughts turning to who might win, who might lose, how, and why. Any social development programme involves the distribution of status, influence and authority within a power context. This is the stuff of politics, especially when one considers that many programmes try to maintain a high level of public visibility and invariably are subject to pressures of all sorts from many directions.
>
> (Graycar 1983: 173)

Study Activity 4

In what way(s) might policy evaluation be seen as a political process? Give some examples of the relationship between tourism policy and politics

CONCLUSION

The policy-making process is not complete after a policy is implemented. A facet of the policy-making process (and a potentially very political one at that) is the monitoring and evaluating of outcomes against expectations or intended outcomes. In reality, it is a rare thing to see tourism policies critically evaluated, for this requires the commitment of substantial resources, and may pose a considerable threat to various interests in the policy-making process in an arena which is becoming increasingly politicised.

Evaluation does not conclude the tourism policy process. That process is ongoing. Policies and programmes continue (usually in some altered state) or are terminated. If they are terminated, they are replaced in the sense that the resources they tied up are given to some other policy or programme. Some stakeholders will voice concerns about the termination of the policy and their claims may be met, if not entirely. There is no clear beginning or end to policy-making.

DISCUSSION QUESTIONS

1.. Why is the systematic evaluation of tourism policy so often lacking in tourism strategic planning and management?

2. What is meant by the term policy evaluation?

3. Why is it necessary to evaluate tourism policy?

4. What does meaningful policy evaluation involve?

5. Why is it difficult to evaluate tourism policy?

6. What external and internal (organisational) factors can influence policy evaluation?

7. Outline how Graycar's model might be used to evaluate tourism policy.

8. Why are Policy evaluations invariably political?

APPLICATION

Cite any <u>one</u> tourism policy that has been evaluated and subsequently modified.

1. What were the original aims and objectives of this policy directive?

2. How have these been changed?

3. Who (or what bodies/institutions) were responsible for conducting this evaluation?

4. Against what criteria was the policy directive evaluated?

RECOMMENDED READING

Graycar, A (1983) Welfare Politics in Australia, Macmillan, Melbourne.

Hogwood ,B, Gunn, L (1984) Policy Analysis for the Real World; Oxford University Press.

Hollick, M (1993) An Introduction to Project Evaluation; Longman, Cheshire.

Owen, J M (1993) Program Evaluation; Allen and Unwin; St Leonards

Rossi, P H et al (1979) Evaluation: A Systematic Approach, Beverly Hills: Sage.

CHAPTER 9

Establishing Priorities for Action

CHAPTER OUTLINE

Introduction - the problem of prioritisation

Evaluating priorities - The goal attainment matrix
                                Force field analysis
                                PUV Analysis
                                GEC Matrices

Nominal Group Technique and Prioritisation

Conclusion

CHAPTER OBJECTIVES

Having read this chapter and undertaken the necessary study activities you should: understand:

- Why it is necessary to establish policy priorities.

- The difficulties in prioritising policy initiatives.

- The criteria used to evaluate and prioritise tourism policy.

- The rationale behind (and application of) goal attainment matrices.

- Force field analysis as a method of prioritising policy objectives.

- How PUV and GEC Analysis can be used to prioritise policy aims.

- The potential of Nominal Group Technique as a prioritisation method.

INTRODUCTION

Establishing priorities is probably one of the most critical issues for the research manager interested in effective policy planning and management. The experienced decision-maker usually has no difficulty in coming up with numerous potential policy initiatives aimed at increasing destination competitiveness. However as policy formulation is a costly, time consuming and highly uncertain process, the difficulty comes in deciding on which initiatives or programmes to concentrate resources.

Determining policy priorities is seldom simple. Some indications of appropriate priorities are, of course, given by senior managers or through the institutional direction of programmes. However, judgmental decisions by decision-makers are also involved.

EVALUATING PRIORITIES

In establishing policy priorities a goal attainment matrix is often utilised.

In a goal attainment matrix each policy initiative (or goal) is evaluated with respect to how well it satisfies the overall strategic objectives of a tourism development plan (i.e. does it generate the desired economic benefits at an acceptable cost; minimise negative environmental and socio-cultural impacts; and is it realistic to implement). Trade offs between the relative benefits and costs of alternative policies are required to be made by all stakeholders in the policy-making process.

In order to systematically evaluate each goal or policy a matrix technique is often employed. Figure 9.1 illustrates how a goal evaluation matrix might be compiled

The use of a semantic scale focuses attention on the most easily attainable goals, thereby establishing priorities for action. The use of such a technique has been used in policy evaluation in tourist settings as diverse as The Crater Lake National Park (USA) the Maldives Islands and Iceland.

Policy objectives can also be evaluated (and subsequently prioritised) using force field analysis. This analysis consists of listing the driving forces (or policies) that will push a tourism project to success. At the same time the restraining forces that might induce failure are also listed (see Figure 9.2). In a steady state environment driving and restraining forces are in balance. Changes in driving or restraining forces would either individually or collectively cause a shifting in equilibrium towards success or failure.

Establishing policy priorities requires each policy objective to be studied carefully and assessed on risk, technical feasibility, financial cost, return on investment, and the ease of attainment and consequent socio-cultural, environmental and economic impact on host communities.

Figure 9.1   Sample Evaluation Matrix

Evaluation Factor (policies)	EVALUATION RANKING (DEVELOPMENT PLAN(S))			
	Alternative 1	Alternative 2	Alternative 3	Comments
Facilities accessibility				
Builds upon the regions physical historic and socio-cultural resource base				
Develops market ties				
Provides substantial employment and increased income				
Provides substantial net foreign exchange earnings				
Helps develop economically depressed areas				
Does not pre-empt other important resource areas				
Minimises negative socio-cultural impacts				
Helps achieve archaeological/historic site preservation				
Helps revitalise traditional arts and handicrafts				
Is not disruptive to present land use and settlement patterns				
Minimises negative environmental impacts				
Reinforces environmental conservation & park development				
Makes maximum use of existing infrastructure				
Make maximum multi-purpose use of new infrastructure				
Provides opportunity for staging development				

Notes:

1. This list of evaluation factors is only indicative of the type which could be used, and the evaluation factors actually used will depend on the specific development situation. If the plan objectives are complete and specific, they can sometimes be used directly as the factors.

2. The evaluation ranking can be done on a scale of 1 to 5 or 1 to 10 with the upper end of the scale indicating the higher achievement level. The more important factors can be given greater numerical weighting. The comments column is important for noting special situations, for example, substantial employment may be provided by the plan but considerable migration of workers may be required to provide the employment.

Figure 9.2   Force Analysis of Policy Objectives

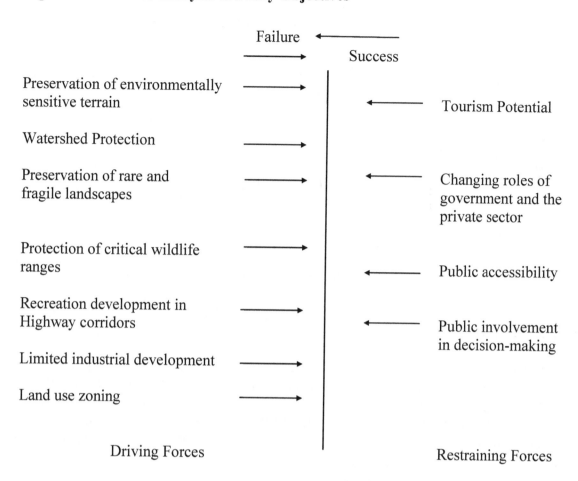

Source: After the future of Kananaskis Country, Alberta, Canada

PUV ANALYSIS

PUV requires that stakeholder attitudes and perceptions towards various policies are mapped on an attitudinal scale. The later is usually expressed by means of an attitudinal approval rating and expressed as a percentage score.

PUV Analysis can either be conducted on individual stakeholder groups or can be completed in totality by all stakeholders with a vested interest in the policy under scrutiny.

In Figure 9.3 the PUV indicates that policy aim three should be given highest priority, closely followed by aims one and four. In this example aims two and five are considered to be the least important and hence given the lowest priority when allocating resources.

Figure 9.3   A Sample PUV Analysis

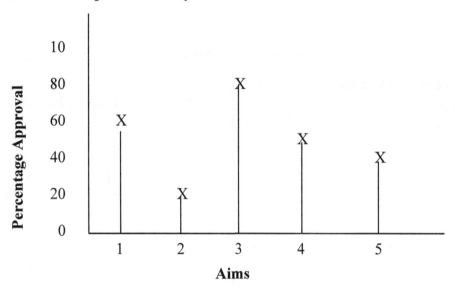

THE GEC MATRIX

GEC matrices can be used to help prioritise policy decisions. In this technique policies are evaluated on the basis of their competitive strengths and market attractiveness. Here policies can be rated as either high medium or low (market attractiveness) or strong medium or weak (competitive strength). Policies are placed in the appropriate category and although there is no automatic strategic prescription, their position is used to help devise an appropriate ranking.

Market attractiveness criteria could include factors such as market growth, profitability, strength of the competition, entry barriers, legal regulation etc. Competitive strength could include technological capability, brand image, production capability and financial strength (to name but a few). The flexibility of the technique is that it can include as many variables as is required. The weakness is that although the matrix is completed by corporate strategists within a company or key policy stakeholders evaluation can be subject to a degree of subjectivity on behalf of the evaluation team e.g. who says, for example, for a carrier to fly a new route entry barriers are low and how do you prove it?

An example of a GEC matrix is given in Figure 9.4. Here the premise is that those policies located towards the top left of the matrix i.e. high competitive strength and market attractiveness are given priority over those that are found gravitating towards the bottom right i.e. low attractiveness and competitiveness.

Figure 9.4   The GEC Matrix

Competitive Strength

	High	Medium	Low
High	Policy 1		
Medium			
Low			Policy 2

(left axis label: **Market Attractiveness**)

In this matrix Policy 1 is given priority over Policy 2

Most users of GEC Matrices recommend that evaluation variables are given a weighting to establish their relative importance, which in turn will reduce the potential for bias. Extreme care is required in making judgements. It also fails to recognise synergies between different policies and businesses e.g. that concentration of ownership is more likely to be accepted as a policy in the aviation industry with movements towards strategic alliances, code sharing and wet/dry leasing.

Study Activity 1

Where have you seen anything like this before?

NOMINAL GROUP TECHNIQUE REVISTED

In Chapter 8 the reader was introduced to NGT as a technique for collecting data on which a policy decision could be undertaken. On closer inspection the more astute student might also realise that as a technique it can also be used for categorising information in order of importance and deriving a consensus on a course of action – a policy decision.

In this context it is not a huge conceptual leap to understand that NGT can be used by policy-makers to collection information on the views of different stakeholders concerning their attitudes towards a range of different policy aims. These aims can then be categorised in order of importance and the information used to prioritise them in order of importance.

Study Activity 2

Try and find an example of where NGT has been used to evaluate various policies in terms of their importance

CONCLUSION

A successful tourism policy might be considered to be one that is soundly established, well resourced, highly regarded and one that is meeting the vision (or overall objectives) of the tourism project. Prioritising for action a number of potentially successful policy initiatives requires an assessment of the corporate objectives of a company or organisation and a trade-off by decision-makers as to the costs and benefits of a range of alternative strategies. Here various techniques such as GEC Matrices and Force Field Analysis can help in making these decisions.

DISCUSSION QUESTIONS

1.   Who (or what bodies) might be involved in prioritising various tourism policies for action?

2.   How are tourism policies prioritised?

3.   Outline the principles behind the use of a goal attainment exercise?

4.   What is force-field analysis? How can it be used to evaluate and prioritise tourism policies?

5.   Distinguish between PUV and GEC Matrices. Which technique, in your views, has the most flexibility when evaluating policy alternatives?

RECOMMENDED READING

Evans, N, Campbell, D and Stonehouse, G (2005) Strategic Management for Travel & Tourism, Chapter 6, Elsevier.

CHAPTER 10

Best Value Procedures and Practice

CHAPTER OUTLINE

Background

Best Value in Practice – The Case of Tourism in the London Borough of Ealing

The Four Key Elements of Best Value – The Four C's

The Review Timetable

What a Review Should Produce

Presenting Outcomes

Monitoring Plans

Conclusion

CHAPTER OBJECTIVES

Having read this chapter and undertaken the various study activities you should be able to:

- Outline what is meant by the term Best Value

- Recognise this to be a statutory duty of public sector organisations in Great Britain

- Understand how to conduct a Best Value Study

- Note what should be produced, to who and over what timescale

- Discuss its relevance to monitoring and evaluating tourism policy in the public sector

BACKGROUND

Best value is a statutory requirement directed at public authorities. It places a duty on public authorities to deliver services to clear standards – of cost and quality – by the most economic, efficient and effective means possible.

The purpose of the best value initiative is to improve the effectiveness and quality of public services. In identifying best practice and ensuring that everyone learns from it in order to improve service provision, best value represents a pertinent example of policy evaluation. It asks the question: are demand and supply strategies the most economic, efficient and effective way of implementing policies?

Implicit in best value procedures is that public authorities publish annual best value performance plans and review all of their strategies every 5 years.

Study Activity 1

Think what this would mean for a NTO or a publicly owned airport/airline.

BEST VALUE IN PRACTICE – THE CASE OF TOURISM IN THE LBE

Ealing Council has adopted a best value framework and a review programme to cover its tourism services since 1999.

The Government has said that in conducting best value reviews, any public authority, including the LBE, should:

- Consider whether it should be providing the service;

- Consider the level at which and the way in which the service is provided;

- Consider the objectives in relation to the provision of the service;

- Assess its performance by reference to any performance indicators (PIs) specified for the service;

- Assess the competitiveness of its performance by comparison with other authorities, commercial and other businesses including voluntary sector organisations;

- Consult other best value authorities, commercial and other businesses and voluntary sector organisations;

- Assess its success in meeting any performance standard which applies in relation to the service;

- Assess progress towards meeting any relevant performance standard which has been specified but which does not yet apply;

- Assess its progress towards meeting any relevant performance target.

Ealing Council expects its tourism services to:

- Meet national standards and demonstrate performance in the top quartile of comparable authorities on the basis of national PIs or set out how they will achieve this in their improvement plan;

- Consistently meet Ealing's customer standards for 2002 on access, opening hours, answering telephone calls and dealing with correspondence and complaints;

- Subject to a range of local standards and PIs which complement national PIs and can be compared with other providers;

- Demonstrate their achievement of The Commission for Racial Equality's "Quality Means Equality" standards and LA21 plan targets;

- Produce efficiency improvements of at least 2% per year;

- Compare favourably with alternative providers or other authorities in terms of costs;

- Subject to the standards set by award schemes and external quality marks.

Study Activity 2

What would you include under the category 'tourism services'?

THE FOUR KEY ELEMENTS OF BEST VALUE – THE 4 Cs

Whilst reviews may approach their work in different ways, four key elements must be addressed in any best value evaluation. These are to:

❏ Challenge   Why the particular service(s) is/are needed at all, and whether it needs to be provided in any particular form.

❏ Compare   Performance with others across a range of relevant indicators, taking into account the views of both service users and potential suppliers.

❏ Consult   With local taxpayers, service users and other stakeholders in the setting of service standards and new performance targets.

❏ Compete   In the sense of demonstrating competitiveness on price and quality by whatever means a service is delivered.

REVIEW TIMETABLE

Any review will follow a predetermined timetable. An example of such a timetable is provided in table 10.1. Tasks (often referred to as milestones) are listed in a left hand column. Key tasks are indicated in some way. In this case, by the use of asterisks (**). Tasks are then programmed over a calendar year (or years). Key actions incorporated under each specific task are provided in checklists 1-7.

WHAT A REVIEW SHOULD PRODUCE

What will emerge from a review will depend very much on the service being reviewed and the approach taken by the review team. Nevertheless, all reviews should produce:

-       A detailed analysis of the service, explaining how it is provided, what changes are needed to the way it is structured and why, and how these changes are to be brought about.

-       An analysis of alternative provision, or where changes are not envisaged, how the service will continue to demonstrate that it is the most effective means of provision.

-       Whether local and national standards for the service are being met.

-       An account of the views of service users and stakeholders.

Study Activity 3

How might you do this?

-       An improvement plan, showing how the service will achieve a 2% annual efficiency improvement.

-       A set of long-term goals for the service.

-       A set of well defined performance indicators and targets that will measure economy, efficiency and effectiveness.

-       A clear audit trail showing exactly how performance information will be collected and recorded.

-       An assessment of how and when progress will be reported to all stakeholder groups.

PRESENTING OUTCOMES

Improvement plans, once complete, are presented to the following groups of individuals.

•   'Scrutineers' (An objective third-party)

•   Senior management (Director and Assistant Director responsible for the service)

•   Staff in the service

•   A nominated trade union representative

•   The best value task group (the group who conducted the exercise).

A reduced (or summarised) copy of the plan together with a formal presentation of proposals is given to an executive. The Executive consists of senior management drawn from the authority as a whole, elected and non-elected members (in the case of a local authority councillors and representatives form central government). It is the Executive that agrees any improvement plan and specific targets identified therein.

MONITORING PLANS

All service providers are expected to monitor their performance in addition to BVPP. Typically this is done quarterly by senior management. Monitoring is a requirement of all local authority service providers – both in-house and those put out to tender.

CONCLUSION

This chapter provides an introduction to best value procedures and practices. It identifies the government's four C's (challenge, compare, consult and compete) as a bass for best value review and explains the process of conducting a such a review.

RECOMMENDED READING

HMSO, (1998) Modernising Local Government: Improving Local Services through Best Value.

LBE, (2000) Best Value. Good Practice Guidelines for Managers.

APPLICATION

Much is currently made in the media of the concept of sustainability. In responding to Local Agenda 21 the many Borough's in London have adopted Best Value Practices and Procedures.

What have been the Key Performance Indicators either used by the various London Borough's in monitoring their performance as a sustainable service providers? Over what timescales will their review plans be undertaken and what stakeholders will be involved in the review process?

Table 10.1   A Review Time Table for a Best Value Study

KEY	TASKS/MILESTONES	Apr	Ma	Jun	Jul	Au	Sep	Oct	Nov	Dec	Jan	Feb	Mar	Apr	Ma	Jun	Jul	Au	Sep	Oct	Nov	Dec	Jan	Feb	Mar	See check list
											2001												**2002**			
	Establish review team and assign tasks		■																							1
	Review current position			■	■																					2
***	Prepare scope and terms of reference				■	■	■	■	■	■																
***	Produce baseline information				■	■	■	■	■	■																
***	Prepare gap analysis								■	■																
***	Establish detailed project plan									■																
***	Challenge	■	■	■	■	■	■	■	■	■	■	■	■													3
	Consult	■	■	■	■	■	■	■	■	■	■	■	■													4
	Compare										■	■	■													5
	Compete										■	■	■													6
***	Produce report and 4 year improvement plan								■	■																7

150

Table 10.2   Review Team & Tasks

		Task	Lead Officer	Timescale	Signed Off	Date
1		Establish team and review leader	MD	May-00		
2		Designate responsibility for project planning and management				
3		Identify key tasks and assign	JB	May-00		
4		Decide links between tasks and order of activity				
5		Establish methodology for controlling and monitoring completion of tasks	JB			
6		Identify budget for the review				
7		Identify corporate support wanted, extent and availability	JB			
8		Identify external support required				
9		Identify software requirements eg MS Project				
10		Set out proposed methods and timescales for consultation	MD			
11		Agree arrangements for consulting staff and TUs	MD			
12		Agree arrangements for assessing impact on the environment	MD			
13		Agree monitoring and reporting arrangements for project team, Best Value Group (BVTG) and Cabinet	JB			

Table 10.3   Review Current Position

	Task	Lead Officer	Timescale	Signed Off	Date
1	Location, number, structure, support staff, consultants	JA			
2	Any statutory requirements	MD			
3	Client and provider elements	MD/YJ			
4	Client and contractor arrangements, services out to contract or other provider	MD/YJ			
5	Similar or complimentary services provided by independent/voluntary sectors	MD/YJ			
6	Strategic statement - Objectives - Service standards - Service plans	MD			
7	Budgets for salaries, operational, capital, physical assets, overheads, income	JB			
8	Major trends in budgets over the last 2-3 years and impact on services: - Kept within budget and met financial targets - Major variances, reasons and impact - Unit costs and trends if applicable	JB			
9	Major net budget commitments and planned investment over next 2-3 years	MD			
10	Changes that will affect service delivery in the future - Changes in legislation - External circumstances - Changes in customer needs - Demography - Technology - Council policies	MD			
11	Service performance - National Pis - Audit Commission indicators - Local indicators - Boroughwide survey - Local surveys - Benchmarking studies - Customer complaints/ombudsman enquiries - Audit - Levels of sickness absence - Training provided For the above, indentify any trends or major issues and the action taken	JA			

Review Current Position cont/d........

		Task	Lead Officer	Timescale	Signed Off	Date
12		Working practices and methods of service delivery – written and customer and practice	MI			
13		Users of service - Profile by main characteristics - Changes in users and impact on service delivery - Target groups – how successful has the service been in reaching these groups - Potential users not provided for - Trends in usage with implications for the future - Disadvantaged groups users/potential users - Extra income generation	MD			
14		Has service been subject to review, VFM or efficiency study, findings and recommendations, actions taken	MD			
16		Inter relationship with other services and support units	MD			
17		How are staff and TU reps currently involved in decision making	MD			
18		Staff and TU views of current service provision	MD			
19		EMAS delivery targets and other environmental assessments of service carried out and results	MI			
20		Special issues of equality and service diversity that influence service delivery	MD/YJ			
21		Requirements of:- - Disability Discrimination Act - Health & Safety Act - Race Relations Act - Equal Opportunities Act	JA			
22		Implications of single status employment				
23		Adopt national quality standard (ISO9002, IIP, Business Excellence)	MI			
24		Identify existing networks, establish new	YJ			

Table 10.4 Challenge

	Task	Lead Officer	Timescale	Signed Off	Date
1	Identify in detail how the service is provided, by whom, and at what cost				
2	Consider why the service has developed into its current structure and what pressures and decisions have brought this about				
3	Consider whether the service is needed at all, and why				
4	Identify what corporate objectives the service helps the Council to meet				
5	Consider whether the service could be provided differently, either by the Council or another provider				
6	Consider how innovative and alternative ways of providing the service could lead to a more effective service that better meets the needs of its users				
7	Challenge the ways in which services are currently delivered				
8	Identify whether the service meets the standards and targets set by the Council, especially in relation to equality, the environment, healthy living and customer service, and how it can achieve them				
9	Identify changes in the service and demands for the service that are likely within the next 4-5 years				
10	Produce long-term goals and targets for the service				

Table 10.5   Consult

	Task	Lead Officer	Timescale	Signed Off	Date
1	Identify stakeholders				
2	Undertake regular consultation with the groups identified on standards of service, performance levels and targets set in the service's performance plan				
3	Consult users and stakeholders on improvement options and any trade-off between quality and cost				
4	Develop a programme of regular consultation that incorporates a variety of consultation methods (both quantitative and qualitative) and is appropriate to reach all the identified groups stakeholders				
5	Find out why people "self-exclude" from services, and how the service could be improved to meet their needs				
6	Take account of the views of councillors in their role as community representatives				
7	Take account of the views of staff and relevant trade unions				
8	Use suggestions and complaints that have been recorded from service users and staff				
9	Develop performance indicators for public satisfaction with your services and monitor these regularly as outcome performance measures				
10	Develop a programme to publish performance against national and local standards in a variety of media that reaches all groups of stakeholders				

Table 10.6   Compare

	Task	Lead Officer	Timescale	Signed Off	Date
1	Document the way the service is currently organised and measured				
2	Investigate and understand the full range of standards and targets that may apply to the service – this includes targets set within the department, by the Council, by the Government or Audit Commission or by appropriate professional bodies				
3	Assess performance against existing service standards, performance indicators (Pis) and targets				
4	Ensure that performance data is accurate, consistent, well-defined and properly documented				
5	Compare your service to other similar local authorities, as well as other public and voluntary bodies and private sector				
6	Consider how the scope of comparisons can be expanded beyond national performance indicators and currently available data eg using benchmarking clubs				
7	Consider what new local performance indicators are needed to reflect the scope and range of the service, and how it performs and take account of users' views on suitable Pis				
8	Demonstrate that you have considered information derived from performance indicators and used it to improve service performance and set targets				

Table 10.7   Compete

		Task	Lead Officer	Timescale	Signed Off	Date
1		Compare costs with other councils and public service providers				
2		Look for benchmarking groups which can share more detailed cost information				
3		Develop appropriate unit cost measures for the service, in particular ones which can be used to make comparisons with other providers				
4		Identify elements of the service that can be compared with the private and voluntary sectors				
5		Consider what aspects of the service could be subject to price testing through competitive tendering				
6		Research the market for service providers and assess how effective a competitive tendering exercise would be at reducing unit costs of a service while maintaining quality and coverage of the service				
7		Develop a more detailed programme of market testing where services appear to be providing poor value for money as part of the service improvement plan, as well as proposals to reduce costs in the short term				
8		Identify the scope for alternative provision and whether there are cost benefits with any of the alternative models				

CHAPTERS 6-10

A REVIEW

Chapters 6-10 have concentrated on the how research and research activity can be a tool used by policy-makers to not only make policy, but also evaluate the success of any policy. Here it has been shown that both primary and secondary data can be used to make policy decisions while both quantitative and qualitative research approaches are frequently used when evaluating policy decisions.

Before we move ahead it is important that you should be able to:

- Explain how research is an important tool used by policy-makers in formulating policy aims and objectives

- Outline the process of conducting research

- Understand what makes 'good' research and hence a good policy decision

- Identify the need for evaluating tourism policy

- Discuss prescriptive and descriptive methods that might be used to evaluate various types of tourism policy

- Be conversant in the use of a range of evaluative techniques that could be applied to policies in both the public and private sectors.

The Concept of Mega Policy

A Study of EU Aviation Policy

CHAPTER 11

The Concept of Mega Policy

The Development of EU Aviation Policy

CHAPTER OUTLINE

Introduction

The Problems of Developing a European Aviation Policy

Mega Policy

Examining EU Aviation Policy

The Complexity of EU Aviation Policy

EU Aviation Policy

CHAPTER OBJECTIVES

Having read this chapter and undertaken the necessary study activities you should understand:

- What is meant by the term Mega-policy

- How EU aviation policy can be seen as an example of mega-policy

- The problems of implementing mega-policies

- The complexity of EU aviation mega-policy

- How it might be possible to evaluate the success or otherwise of such a policy initiative.

INTRODUCTION

On the 25th March 1957 six countries – France, West Germany, Italy, Belgium, Luxembourg and the Netherlands – signed the Treaty of Rome. This committed themselves to forming a European Economic Community (EEC), the forerunner of today's European Union (EU).

The European Economic Community was based on four common or founding policies. These were a common agricultural policy, a common external trade policy, a common transport policy and a common competition policy. These common policies came to be known as the four founding 'Pillars' of the EEC. Incorporated under the heading of transportation, aviation has consequently a long history of European control and intervention in its practices.

This said, it has been noted that policy in this area is somewhat fragmented and piecemeal (IATA 2004). Indeed Akhurst (2007) has described European aviation policy as 'an amorphous mass of disparate ideas' implying that it is all over the place.

This chapter will question why this is the case? In doing so it will question whether:

- The EU is not simply interested in civil aviation (an assumption that is clearly questionable given its interest in open skies agreements)

- As an industry could it be that aviation is very difficult to control? Within the EU currently we are dealing with 26 member states (shortly to become 27) all of whom have different national interests and different political systems. In each country aviation plays a differing degree of importance in their national economies. To make the situation more complicated each member state also contains a number of registered airlines some of which are private sector national flag carriers and others publicly owned

- Finally we are dealing with an industry with a number of powerful and influential stakeholders all representing the interests of their members airlines. Foremost among these are bodies such as IATA, AEA, ICAO et al

THE PROBLEMS OF DEVELOPING A EUROPEAN AVIATION POLICY

It is against this backdrop that the European Union has attempted to produce a coherent and workable aviation policy.

The European Union is itself a product of a Treaty – The 1992 Treaty on European Union – more commonly referred to as the Maastricht Treaty. This treaty committed member states, amongst other things, to a European Transport Union. In this union members would enjoy the free movement of goods services persons and capital. Markets would be open and barriers to trade eliminated. For the European aviation industry Maastricht heralded the start of a new dawn; a dawn that promised 'open skies' and a deregulated aviation industry.

Study Activity 1

Davidson, R (2005) contains a good chapter on the growth of the European Union and formal mechanisms for producing and implementing European legislation.

Having read Davidson you are encouraged to undertake the following tasks.

1. *At the time of publication the EU contains twenty six member states. Name them and note when they joined the Union.*

2.	*The EU is not only a diverse geographical area (from Nordic countries to those bordering the Mediterranean) but also contains countries with widely differing political systems. Choose any three member states and examine how their government's political ideologies differ. For example, you might care to compare France Germany and Great Britain all currently with socialist governments but with widely differing interpretations of socialist principles.*

3.	*In a region of widespread economic and cultural differences from differences in comparative wealth to differing languages, histories, food and drink, music and even attitudes to religion; it is inevitable that there will always be longstanding prejudices, nationalist tensions and mistrust between member states. Provide some examples of where such differences have recently surfaced in European history. Consider how these might cause problems for policy-making.*

So how realistic then is to expect that we will ever produce a common European aviation policy? At the risk of sounding glib, the answer to this question is that perhaps you have to start somewhere. Indeed, out of the ashes of war in 1945 who would have ever believed that Germany and Poland or Germany and France would ever have established diplomatic relations let alone work together and share a common European parliament?

MEGA POLICY

This chapter requires that you consolidate your knowledge from earlier chapters.

In Chapter 1, for example, it was noted that policy can be made on a variety of different organisational levels something we referred to as a policy hierarchy. Within this hierarchy policy can be made at the company, town, district, region, country or even international level. Throughout this text various examples of policy taken from different levels in the policy hierarchy have been discussed.

In Chapter 4 it was noted that policy made at the international level is referred to by Ritchie (1997) as Mega-policy. Here we are talking about a set of rules, regulations, guidelines or directives that span international boundaries. In this context, EU aviation policy fits into this category.

EXAMINING EU AVIATION POLICY

There remains a simple way of keeping up to date on all new EU policy directives in this area. It is called the Air transport portal of the European Commission. The portal covers issues, policies and press releases from the EU and broaches topics as diverse as airport planning and development, safety, security, competition policy and the impact of aviation on the environment (amongst others).

The astute reader will check it on a weekly basis at www.ec.europa.eu/transport/air_portal

Apart from being informed, for the student of policy studies there is another good reason for checking the portal. As noted in Chapter 4, the first step in making policy is always to determine what is possible, legal, ethical or socially responsible. Either rightly or wrongly, increasingly for those of us who live in Europe or who have dealings with Europe, the EU is laying down the 'rules of the game'. They dictate what is possible in business. As such, any policy-maker or corporate strategist ignores the dictates of the EU at their peril.

THE COMPLEXITY OF EU AVIATION POLICY

There is a world of difference between producing a simple customer relations policy for an individual airline and that governing an entire transport sector for a whole region. While the former might cover how you dress, how you speak to clients and handle any complaints the latter must cover 330 scheduled airlines (169 from within the EU and 161 from outside) as well as 488 airports handling scheduled traffic.

EU Aviation Policy covers over 400 million passengers (a figure expected to double by 2020) IATA World Air Transport Statistics. As such any rules, regulations, guidelines or directives have to be acceptable to all stakeholders and be enforceable across an entire geographical region and sector of the travel industry.

This is clearly a massive task.

EU AVIATION POLICY

It is to the analysis of EU Aviation Policy that attention is now turned. In the ensuing two chapters it will be shown that in this area where individual policies are continually being defined and redefined. As such the subject represents a good example to illustrate the dynamics of the policy-making process.

DISCUSSION QUESTIONS

1.   What is meant by the term mega-policy?

2.   How might EU aviation policy represent a good example of mega-policy?

3.   Why might producing and implementing a piece of mega-policy prove so much harder than that for other policies at different levels in the policy hierarchy?

RECOMMENDED READING

Akehurst, G (2007) Tourism Policies in EU Member States, Mansell, London

Davidson, R (2005) Tourism in Europe, Longman

CHAPTER 12

EU Internal Aviation Policy

CHAPTER OUTLINE

Internal and external aviation policy

Internal policy – basic principles

a.   The EU and Licensing

b.   Relaxing restrictions on the foreign ownership of airlines

c.   The standardisation of operating practices

      i.   Air Traffic Control
      ii.   Safety and Security
      iii.   Aircraft Insurance
      iv.   Working Conditions
      v.   Passenger Protection
      vi.   Delays
      vii.   Competition Policy
      viii.   Mergers and Alliances
      ix.   Environmental Policy
      x.   Airport Proposals

Conclusions

CHAPTER OBJECTIVES

Having read this chapter and undertaken the necessary study activities you should understand:

- The two components of EU aviation policy, namely internal and external policy

- What EU internal aviation policy hopes to achieve

- Some of the problems of implementing an internal aviation mega-policy within the European Union

INTERNAL AND EXTERNAL AVIATION POLICY

EU aviation policy incorporates two components.

- One governing EU registered airlines (e.g. BA, Air France etc) flying within the EU – *EU internal aviation policy*

- One governing non-EU registered airlines (e.g. United, Air Canada, Thai, Emirates) who seek permission to fly into EU air space – *EU external aviation policy*

INTERNAL AVIATION POLICY – BASIC PRINCIPLES

'The basic aim of the EU is to achieve a safe, affordable, convenient and efficient service for consumers. We believe the best way to achieve this goal is to allow unrestricted fair competition that will determine variation in quality, price and service'.

Daniel Calleja. Director Designate, Air Transport Directorate (2004)

The aforementioned quote from Calleja sums up internal aviation policy in a nutshell. However, how might providing a safe, affordable, convenient and cheap service be achieved? This takes our discussion into the realms of aircraft licensing, safety and security measures and aviation insurance (to mention but a few).

The EU and Licensing

Traditionally for airlines to operate a service between member states they have needed an operating licence. This has been granted by individual member states. New proposals put forward by the EU, transfers this power from individual governments to Brussels.

Such proposals have been incorporated under the auspices of EU Competition policy. They are at the corner stone of EU transport policy.

Study Activity 1

In this context, what advantages might be generated by transferring power from member states to Brussels?

Relaxing restrictions on foreign ownership of airlines

EU internal aviation policy proposes a truly competitive aviation industry where the laws of the free market determine such factors as service providers, price and levels of service quality. Believers in the market economy have often maintained that government intervention distorts the market and prevents the efficient provision of services. It is a comparatively small step to take this argument further and allow 'foreign' or other EU member states airlines unrestricted access to internal (EU) markets opening up the possibility of direct competition on routes and a price war. In such situations only the strongest survive and small inefficient airlines 'go to the wall'.

How you read the situation depends on your political point of view. On the face of it competition sounds good if it results in cheaper fares and more profitable airlines. However, the deregulation experiment in the US suggested that for some basic public utilities, such as civil aviation, maybe some form of regulation is desirable.

Study Activity 2

What actually happened in the US? Why might some form of EU regulation be desirable? Indeed how might it happen?

Standardisation of operating practices

The argument goes does it make sense to have 26 countries each with separate rules and regulation governing the operation of their civil aviation industries?

The EU maintains that the answer to this question is no.

So what does the EU propose?

1. Air traffic control

Launched as an idea by the EU in October 2002 and ratified by members in principle in 2003, the EU proposes the *Single European Sky initiative (EC550/2004)*

This proposal argues for a unified European air traffic control system administered by the organisation EUROCONTROL. Under the scheme European air space will be restructured (with a movement away from air route networks based on borders) to something reflecting traffic flows. Capacity will be increased and the system will designed to be more efficient (with less bureaucracy and consequent cost savings)

Individual Air Traffic Controllers (ATC's) will be replaced by a number of regional command & control centres or charging zones covering much larger areas. In GB there will be two. One in Scotland for en-route transatlantic traffic and one at Swanwick, Hampshire controlling Southern England & the Channel

The deadline for the completion of the scheme is to be 2020

Linked to these regulations is the policy (EC550/2004 Article 15) that there should be a *common charging scheme* for ATC services. Charging zones will be established in the EU and airlines will pay a flat fee for each zone they pass through. The charging formula will reflect the different nature of services (i.e. you would pay more a 777 than a 737 and more for a long-haul service as opposed to a short-haul one). Fees for the service will be collected by individual states or by EUROCONTROL

These regulations do not apply to aerodromes with less than 10,000 commercial take-offs & landings p.a. (calculated over a three year period). Here ATC's can take responsibility for their own aircraft however they have to notify the EC that they will operate outside of the system. Also exempt from charging will be aircraft less than 2 tons and flights on official missions by reigning Monarchs, Heads of State/governments and government ministers. Potentially exempt are Military flights, training flights, test flights & VFR flights

156

Study Activity 3

Do you see any potential problems here?

In 2007 the EU Transport Commissioner noted ATC understaffing (by as much as 50% in some countries). In addition he observed cost overruns and delays to major projects. Swanwick in the UK for example is currently running 7 years late and costs have increased from £462-750 million. Added to this has been poor dialogue between ATC's and national governments. Indeed in some cases this has expressed itself as open conflict between governments and ATC's (the latter concerned about the privatisation of services or decisions to run ATC as a PPP's).

Operational problems have only compounded the situation e.g. 17/6/00 when all the computers went down at NATS (UK). Staff have complained that they have not been involved in the technical evolution of systems. Added to this because military airspace will be outside the control of EUROCONTROL there will be the need for co-ordinating mechanisms governing the use of civilian and military airspace.

2. Safety & Security

The EU recognises that providing a safe & secure transport system is of the utmost priority for the air transport industry.

- **Security**

EU proposals concerning aviation security are outlined in document COM (205) 429. This addresses the need for consultation with interested stakeholders; risk assessment; funding of new security measures; proposals for one-stop security control and comitology.

Consultation measures propose the establishment of a Stakeholders' Advisory Group on Aviation Security (SAGAS) to advise the EU, European Commission and member states on the technical & operational details of implementing any new security measures.

Regarding *Risk Assessment*, SAGAS will assess the nature of the risk, the effectiveness of existing security measures and the impact of any measures proposed.

Funding security measures propose this should be jointly shared by both the aviation industry and national governments.

One stop Security advocates passengers, baggage, cargo and aircraft having undergone the necessary security controls at one EU airport, need not repeat these when transferring through another EU airport. Article 17 of this document also proposes extending this to third countries (beyond the EU). Where necessary individual member states will have the powers to determine whether any additional security measures are necessary e.g. the UK liquid ban of August 2006.

Comitology argues that these principles should be non-negotiable, sensitive information should not be made public and best practice will be shared among member states.

As with so many aspects of EU aviation policy problems remain. Certain sovereign states have expressed a wish to retain their rights to legislate as they see fit on matters pertaining to security. This raises the issue is security an EU or national issue?

Related to this is the question who should pay for increased security measures - the airlines or national governments?

The EU's view is that enhanced levels of security should be paid for by the following means:

- An aviation security tax imposed by governments
- Security surcharges or fees levied on your tickets
- An airport security charge paid out of airport profits
- State grants and/or subsidies

They have consistently argued against the cost of increased security being passed onto airlines instead seeing this as this is a national security issue.

Study Activity 4

What is your view here?

- **Safety**

The international nature of the aviation industry calls for an international approach to safety regulation. Traditionally this has been the responsibility of ICAO

However for 30 years the EU has (and continues) to operate in this area.

It does this through the work of various Joint Aviation Authorities (JAA) all working together, for example, the CAA in the UK. Their work has been incorporated into European law

To simplify things and produce some common standards the EU proposes to introduce a pan-European Aviation Safety Authority (EASA). This will have legal powers to impose the standards it adopts

The EU endorses the work of the *European Civil Aviation Conference* (a grouping of 41 European countries) and their work to assess the *Safety of Foreign Aircraft* (EU policy EC2006/474). This proposed that governments doubled their budgets to undertake targeted and random spot checks on airlines where they have specific safety concerns.

Where these airlines fail to meet airworthiness standards the EU will seek a withdrawal of their permits to fly in EU air space. To date 16 different airlines have fallen foul of this legislation including airlines such as Phuket Airlines, Nigerian Airlines and all airlines registered in the Democratic of the Congo, Indonesia & Equatorial Guinea, Swaziland, Sierra Leone & the Kyrgz Republic .

Other airlines like PIA are allowed to fly into EU airspace providing they us wet leased air craft obtained from an airline not subject to the ban

Airlines on the 'banned list' can be found on the EU aviation portal.

Study Activity 5

How affective have these measures been?

To date, no one JAA & its policies have legal status within the EU. National variations in standards also remain. It has been shown that cumbersome committee structures and the need to achieve consensus can cause delay decision-making. On the other hand JAA's like the CAA are worried that the new EASA might undermine its work, while the standards it imposes might not be as strict as those currently adopted in the UK. There is also some evidence to suggest that individual governments have tried to interfere with the work of the EASA.

3. Aircraft Insurance

There remains a fundamental problem relating to the need to insure aircraft, passengers and their crew. This revolves around the fact that the largely London-based insurance market has threatened to withdraw from providing cover for airlines by adding exclusion clauses to policies. Here if the airline is attacked by weapons of mass destruction (radiological, biological, chemical, electronic etc) airlines are waking up to the fact that both passengers they carry and the aircraft they use are potentially not covered for any loss or damage.

Since 2004 the EU has insisted that any aircraft either flying over European airspace or landing at a European airport must obtain war risk coverage (that also covers terrorist acts). This has forced the airlines to self insure.

The reluctance of the insurance market to cover certain airlines on certain routes and a failure of ICAO to come up with a solution to this problem has meant that the EU has been forced to accept government backed coverage for uninsurable risks

Again problems are only too evident in this policy. British Airways in their 2007 Annual Report to shareholders have questioned whether European airlines should also hold third party liability? (i.e. if one of them is shot down and causes losses on the ground these people will also be covered). Extending the argument, it is questionable whether airport authorities also carry this insurance? (For example, to protect against a Glasgow incident).

It is possible to question whether there will there be a cap on total liability? This ponders whether there will there be a limit to the risk that insurers are prepared to accept? For example, American aircraft on-route from the Middle-East flying over EU airspace – are they an unacceptable risk?

If there is to be a cap, the argument goes who should pay for this extra risk insurance? We have seen governments have stepped in but the EU believes this should be funded by a tax on ticket prices. Naturally the airlines disagree believing they are already taxed too much

Clearly we have not heard the last on this issue

Study Activity 6

Do you perceive the risk of flying on a US carrier is greater than that of an EU registered airline? As such could increased premiums on these airlines be considered to be acceptable?

4. Working Conditions

The EU proposes to extend the working time directive to mobile staff in aviation primarily by imposing flight time limitations. While in its own right any attempt to improve the terms and conditions of service of staff must be welcomed, for airlines the problem will be maintaining a balance between being fair to staff, pursuing a policy of operational safety and guaranteeing the economic interests of investors.

Study Activity 7

You may care to look at the EU working time directive in a little more detail. What does it propose? How might this have implications for organisational competitiveness?

5. Passenger Protection

There are a number of EU directives that are important here. Together they constitute part of what is internal aviation policy within the European Union.

The most important of these directives is *COM (2000) 365 Protection for Air Passengers in the EU*. This proposes:

- Giving delayed passengers the right to seek re-imbursement or an alternative flight
- Forcing airlines to spell out in a contract their obligations to passengers
- Making airlines release information in order that passengers can make informed choices between different airlines
- Making airlines accept the need to cater for the needs of disabled passengers
- Introducing a simple scheme for passengers to lodge a complaint and settle disputes out of court
- Forcing airports to establish a passenger code of conduct
- Strengthening the representation of passengers on decision-making bodies
- Establishing an airline code of conduct in the area of internet booking practices
- Studying the affects of code sharing on competition
- Assessing the impacts of cabin conditions on passenger health by establishing a number of 'expert' monitoring groups

EU aviation policy also goes further in this area. The *2004 EU-US PNR (passenger name records) Directive* has been a response to the increased terrorist threat. This proposes that all airlines flying to, from and through US airspace should hand over details of their passengers in the form of PNR or passenger name record.

Here the EU has come in for considerable criticism. It has, for example, been challenged by human rights groups in the European Court of Justice. Their claim is that such a scheme is illegal under the 1995 EU Data Protection Directive

For its part the EU has come back with some modifications to the scheme. These include:

- That airlines should submit no more than 34 pieces of information
- No data on special passenger requirements will be sent
- There would be no transfer of data between airlines
- This information would be used in anti-terrorist activity only
- PNR's would be destroyed after 3.5 years

This said, a number of Members of the European Parliament are still not happy. Irrespective of their views the EU has now imposed this scheme by making the directive a Treaty in 2006 thereby giving the directive legal powers

Study Activity 8

While PNR's were originally sought by the US government and US carriers the scheme has now extended into Europe. Which country 'paved the way' here by insisting on PNR's on all flights to its international airports in July 2007?

6. Delays

Delays continue to be a problem that bedevils the aviation industry. Delays result in passenger frustration and can cause serious operational problems to airlines as a result of missing their landing and take-off slots.

As the skies over Europe have become more congested and the time taken to process passengers has increase, largely as a result of the tightening of airport security, so airline delays have become a 'hot' topic for conversation in the world of civil aviation.. As an issue the problems posed by the delay of airline departures and arrivals is something the EU is only too aware of.

Their policy response is outlined in Regulation (EC) 261/2004. It proposes in the event of long delays (two hours or more, depending on the distance of the flight), passengers must in every case be offered free meals and refreshments plus two free telephone calls, telex or fax messages, or emails. Should the time of departure be deferred until the next day, passengers must also be offered hotel accommodation and transport between the airport and the place of accommodation. Where the delay is five hours or longer, passengers may opt for reimbursement of the full cost of the ticket together with, when relevant, a return flight to the first point of departure.

This regulation applies to all airline flights departing from an EU airport or to any airline licensed in the EU if that flight is departing from an airport outside the EU and flying to a destination airport within an EU member state.

Regulation 261/2004 also addresses *Denied Boarding Compensation in the European Community.* This advocates that if you are bumped from a flight within the EU or if you are on an airline registered in the EU and your flight departed outside the EU bound for a destination within the EU, you automatically have the following rights:

- Reimbursement of the cost of the ticket within seven days, a return flight to the first point of departure or re-routing to the final destination;.

- Refreshments, meals, hotel accommodation, transport between the airport and place of accommodation, two free telephone calls, telex or fax messages, or emails;

- Compensation totaling:

    o   250 euros for all flights of 1,500 kilometers or less;

    o   400 euros for all flights within the European Community between 1,500 and 3,500 kilometers;

    o   600 euros for all other flights.

The EU envisage that the scheme will apply to all scheduled, charter and separate tour operator flights. They also believe it will help to reduce the over-booking policy of airlines.

This said problems nevertheless remain. For example, carriers from outside the EU but flying into EU airspace will not have to pay compensation. In addition, what you receive by way of compensation will be determined by individual company policies and an international piece of legislation (the Montréal Treaty). Compensation will not be paid by airlines for extraordinary circumstances. This, of course, raises the issue what is an extraordinary circumstance – strikes, bad weather, a terrorist alert?

The European Regional Airline Association has argued that such a scheme will cost £1.5 billion euros to implement. The also bemoan the fact they were not consulted on the mechanics of such a scheme.

The scheme has also received two legal challenges from the European Low Fares Airline Association and IATA both of whom consider the scheme to be inoperable.

Elsewhere airlines such as Ryan Air have pointed out that potentially they could find themselves in a situation whereby they will be paying out more in compensation than they generate in flight revenue.

Study Activity 9

So what can be said for this directive? Who will be the 'winners' and 'losers' here?

7. Competition Policy

The EU takes a robust stance on competition as witnessed in their Open Skies agreements of 1992, 1994 and 1997. The EU have consistently argued that aviation should be subject to the same European rules on competition as that which governs any other industry.

The various open skies agreements advocated by the Union are based on three principles.

-     That all European airlines can fly between any two community airports and freely decide fares, new routes and capacity

-     Carriers should have the ability to conduct their own ground handling operations and have equal access to infrastructure, facilities and marketing channels

-     And that the opening up of the industry to new competitors should become a reality and not hindered by obstacles such as limits on cross border investments

Here the EU has seen its role as to:

-   Enforce competition rules

-   Develop policies – rules and regulations – that enhance competition

-   Abolish IATA Block Exemption Regulations or standard fares between conference areas

Study Activity 10

To what extent do you believe the EU has been successful in achieving some of these objectives?

Typically we see in EU fines for airlines that receive illegal public subsidies (such as the Irish airline Air Lingus); the insistence that carriers give up some of their take-off and landing slots at their 'Hub Airports' (such as British Airways at London Heathrow) and a wide range of fare options between destinations like Europe and the Far East

The EU also screens all proposals for new routes within, to and from the EU to see that proposals do not encourage or authorise such practices as price or capacity fixing

Study Activity 11

Have they ever found any evidence of price fixing?

The opening up of the skies has allowed new entrepreneurs to become established including many of the new 'no frills' operators and has given more choice to the consumer helping to bring down fares. Page (2005) Indeed, the EU Transport Commissioner speaking at IIASL Conference in Holland in 2007 estimated that fares have fallen in real terms by 30% since 1992 while direct flights between EU airports has doubled.

It has even been prepared to stand-by as member states national airlines go bankrupt (as witnessed with the Belgium national airline Sabina). Despite this, critics would say that state subsidies are still going on and that the EU turns a 'blind eye' to certain illegal practices (as witnessed by the massive public subsidies currently being given to Air Italia and the Polish airline LOT). Elsewhere Air France, it is argued, also gets a subsidy and enjoys a monopoly on the mainland France-Corsica link something Easyjet finds 'hard to believe on such a popular route' (Bachetta GM Easyjet France 2007).

In short despite what the EU might say it remains politically hard for any national government to sit back and watch its national flag carrier go bankrupt with the consequent loss of jobs and dent to national pride. In the past, various French governments have also found a failure to subsidise state enterprises tantamount to 'political suicide'.

Elsewhere liberalisation of the external aviation market is still in its infancy. This includes flights to and from the EU (such as EU & the US or EU & China). The result has been limited market competition & less pressure on airlines to improve the quality of their service and operating efficiency. As a consequence prices can be higher - to the detriment of customers & Europe's overall competitiveness.

8. Mergers & Alliances

The EU is not anti-merger or anti-alliance between EU member airlines providing such mergers/alliances can be shown to enhance efficiency and competitiveness Indeed the EU supported the Air France-KLM and Lufthansa-Swiss initiatives.

Their thinking has been that such agreements:

1.   Can bring important benefits to passengers by connecting networks
2.   Offer new services

3.   Generate efficiencies e.g. code/route sharing

Implicit however is such mergers/alliances *must* generate benefits for passengers. At the same time the EU recognise that airlines have to compete in an global market. Here mergers and alliances often allow airlines to achieve economies of scale.

The EU is on record as saying that it will actively investigate and make a judgement on potential anti-competitive global alliances. Here the current Sky Team Investigation is illustrative. The EU is investigating Sky Teams practices on internal EU routes and those between the EU and third countries

9. Environmental Policy

EU environmental policy with respect to aviation is outlined in the document DG Energy & Transport – Unit F3 Environment & Safety.

The thinking behind this policy is that carbon dioxide (Co2) emissions from the EU aviation industry can contribute to climate change. The science shows Co2 emissions from international aviation increased by 67% between 1990-2002 and is currently increasing by 4.4% p.a. (European Energy Assoc 2004).

ICAO (2005) also predict world passenger traffic will grow by 14% p.a. and freight by 13% with no prospect of a slowing down in growth of the aviation sector. Indeed, the world passenger fleet will double in size by 2020 and any technological improvements in reducing Co2 (by introducing new fuel-efficient aicraft such as the Boeing Dreamliner) will be more than outstripped by aviation growth

Various nightmare scenarios have been put forward as to the consequences of global warming. These include rising sea levels as a consequence of the melting of the polar ice caps, flooding, erosion, extreme weather events and even water shortage in certain parts of the world.

The EU policy response to global warming must be seen as part of a concerted overall strategy. The EU, for example, endorses the *1992 UN Framework Convention on Climate change*. This was agreed by 183 countries at Rio de Janeiro. Here all signatories to a sustainability agenda (Agenda 21) agreed as part of an overall package of measures to cut green house gas emissions as their contribution to climate change.

The events at Rio have subsequently come to be proceeded by the *1997 Kyoto Protocol*. Here 108 countries set the target of reducing 6 greenhouse gasses by 5.2% below 1990 levels by 2012

As part of this protocol the EU is allowed to meet its commitments jointly (5.2% in overall terms). This only serve to disguise the fact that some countries will never achieve this figure, such as Poland while others like the UK will.

Kyoto suggested a number of ways this 5.2% reduction could be achieved. This included technological improvements, joint reduction or regional averaging, through the introduction of 'emissions allowances' and the transfer and trading of unused allowances between companies. (The latter thought to be achievable by 2008). Implicit in the Kyoto Protocol was that these principles were to become legally binding by 15th February 2005.

Specifically in the world of civil aviation the EU has produced a number of its own policy statements. Foremost amongst these has been the *1999 EC Communication on Air Transport and the Environment*

This proposed long term performance targets for airlines with regard to the reduction of green house gasses. The idea was to use of market-based measures to control the problem such as fuel taxes or emissions charges

Other initiatives have included *2000 Towards Meeting the Challenge of Sustainable Development (Green Paper COM:2000:87)*

Here the EU proposed the rejection of ICAOs' policy setting authority. As part of the green paper and an attempt by the EU to set the policy agenda in aviation a number of specific environmental initiatives were put forward. These included new noise proposals. Here the EU proposes establishing new noise standards around populated urban areas with a 30 decibel maximum and no single noise event being louder than 45 decibels. An investigation into why kerosene was zero tax rated & generous public subsidies are given to aircraft manufacturers and purchasers was also advocated. It was felt that the latter factors only helped to subsidise the cost of aircraft travel thereby contributing to the environmental impacts of aviation.

The *2002 EU 6th Environment Action Plan* only served to endorse the 2000 EC Green Paper on greenhouse gas emissions (EU:COM 2000:87 Final). It proposed a CO_2 Green House Emissions Trading Scheme should begin by Jan 2005. Here specific targets and action were to be directed against key polluting industries (of which aviation was one).

The UK has led the way starting the first trading scheme in late 2002. Since then the industry has also commissioned its own studies as to how this might be achieved Arthur Andersen (2001) for IATA and BAA (2003)

On a positive note, as from 1st January 2005 approximately *a* half of all EU CO_2 emissions have been subject to caps under the EU emissions trading scheme. However, as far as aviation goes, currently the sector has no incentive to take account of climate costs for what happens if you exceed your CO_2 target?

Various environmental groups, such as Friends of the Earth, argue that emissions' trading is a soft option and that taxes and direct charges on the airline industry would hurt more. They also maintain that unilateral stands are not enough (such as the £5 UK Green tax on flight seats). Such a scheme needs to be EU wide and considerably more than a couple of pounds.

Study Activity 12

Does the government's green tax put you off using air travel? If not, could it be that this tax is too low? If the tax was to increase ten-fold (to £50) would this make you think more? Indeed is such a tax fair? Does it not discriminate against those people who could least afford to fly?

Perhaps there is also another issue here, namely who should pay the environmental costs of airline travel - the passenger or the airlines?

Not surprisingly some airlines reject the science or refuse to accept any responsibility for their actions. The airline Ryan Air is currently promoting itself as 'The Greenest Airline in the Sky'. Such a clam is based on the somewhat dubious assumptions that their aircraft are some of the most fuel efficient in the skies while their high load factors mean that they are not flying half empty planes. It conveniently ignores the fact that Ryan Airs aircraft fly more often and any fuel savings are more than made up for by continuous operation.

The EU is still waiting on advice from ICAO on how to tackle the problem of green house emissions. Suffice to say that *Friends of the Earth (2005) Growth Scenarios for EU Aviation* believe EU targets based on Kyoto are not enough. They also believe it is not right that some countries are taking great strides to reduce emissions while others are doing very little

They support the findings of the German Federal Environment Ministry who suggest a number of ways forward. These include:

- Common targets to be set across all countries to be achieved by a critical date. *(Does this allow for structural differences between countries and their ability to decrease emissions?)*

- The Triptych Approach with targets linked to per capita income, living standards or GDP *(This assumes the rich countries are the biggest net polluters. Are they?)*

- A multi-stage approach with a variety of different targets or thresholds linked to different stages *(This would certainly soften the pain and make the achievement of certain targets that much more realistic)*

- Different targets for different industries *(This would of course raise the question who decides the targets and against what criteria? Possibly aviation would feel hard done-by compared to other sectors like railway travel or manufacturing)*

- A combination of the above

Other options are discussed at www.fiacc.net/app/approachlist.htm . This offers the interesting idea that targets should be set according to a countries historical contribution to global temperature change. Under such a scheme Great Britain and countries that went through the industrial revolution in the early C19th would not do so well compared to some of the more 'newly industrialising' nations.

Perhaps there are better ways forward in terms of reducing the environmental impacts of aviation? More fuel efficient planes for example such as the Boeing 787, Bio-fuels & hydrogen engines or improving public awareness and changing attitudes to air travel?

Study Activity 13

Has anything been tried here?

The Intergovernmental Panel on Climate Change (1999) Aviation and the Global Atmosphere, ICAO and the *UK's Dept for Transport (2004) White Paper on The Future of Air Transport* have considered these alternative solutions to cutting green house gas emissions.

Their conclusions have been not to expect any radical changes in thinking here. Aircraft design will continue to be based around conventional technologies with elements of best practice being incorporated as the years go by. This said, we can expect aircraft to become more fuel efficient by around 2% p.a. up until 2030. Nitrogen dioxide reduction is expected to be 80% over the same period. Neither however will compensate for the increase in aviation growth. The IPCC also note because of the long life expectancy of today's aircraft – up to 50 years – replacement rates are low and the fuel efficiency of fleets will only increase slowly.

Is hydrogen fuel an alternative? Certainly as a fuel it is less polluting as the by-product of burning hydrogen is water. However this would require major changes in aircraft design and the storage and handling of hydrogen at airports. Planes would have to carry 2.5 times more liquid hydrogen than the same amount of kerosene. Planes would therefore have to be bigger and consequently produce more drag. The solution would be lighter airframes and flying at higher altitude. This presents material design problems and rules out the possibility of using these aircraft on short-haul trips.

In a similar vein could 'Blended Wing Technology' be an alternative? The Cranfield College of Aeronautics suggests that it might be. Here you essentially have a flying wing with the interior of the wing becoming the passenger cabin. Here possibilities to reduce drag and weight can lead to potential fuel efficiency savings of 30%. NASA research (2002) has also shown such aircraft are capable of travelling 7,000 miles in one stretch with load capacities of 450-800 passengers.

Where is the British government going? Here it is useful to examine the views of a number of influential stakeholders who influence Labour Party policy. One such group is the SRA. (*SERA 2007 EU Sustainable Aviation Policy – Lost in Translation*).

The SRA recognise that the industry is under attack from some high-profile NGO's including bodies like Friends of the Earth & Airport Watch. It believes the airline industry is hoping to secure the weakest possible EU emissions trading settlement in the belief that this will prevent any aviation tax increases. At the same time it has also continually try to postpone the setting of any credible EU emissions targets. SRA argue that non CO_2 targets seem to be totally ignored including nitrogen dioxide emissions and noise levels.

SRA maintain if the EU accepts the current rate of aviation growth it simply can not achieve its long term objective of a maximum global temperature change of 2 degrees above pre-industrial levels.

What needs to be done? SRA suggests that the EU needs to accept there is a problem here. They need to recognise that we need some credible targets in-line with Kyoto that apply to all industries (including aviation). These targets should equally apply to carriers coming into European air space as well as domestic operators. Airports as well as airlines should be incorporated into any emissions scheme. SRA note that Arlanda Airport in Stockholm has had a CO_2 cap for sometime and this has effectively limited the growth of this airport. In Great Britain this could be done by one of two ways:

1.   Each airport would have an emissions charge. This would vary according to the aircraft engine and type

2.   A supplement to airport charges would apply to all EU airports. This could be extended to include nitrogen dioxide (NO_2) and noise emissions

Finally the SERA recommend an increase in airport passenger duty. It supports a Franco-German idea that airlines bid at auction for aviation emissions units and these are not just given away free to every airline

Study Activity 14

So what might these proposals mean for aviation policy in this country? How might these ideas be incorporated into EU aviation policy?

10. Airport Proposals

EU internal aviation policy also covers various rules, regulations, guidelines and directives covering the development and operation of airports within member states. Here policy broaches on issues as diverse as slot allocation to airport charging.

- ### Slot Allocation

Here EU proposals are in their infancy. This said, the EU is talking about changing the way slots are allocated at airports. *(European Commission Slot Allocation Consultation 2007/2842)*

The EU estimate that by 2025 as many as 3.7million fights will not be able to take place because of capacity constraints. Their aim is to achieve a more efficient use of airport capacity – thereby preventing airlines not making use of their allocated slots and to open airports up to greater competition.

Proposals' regarding the more efficient use of airport capacity argues for a 10% redistribution of 'grandfather rights'. This would mean carriers would be forced to sell these slots or have them confiscated by the Union. Slots would go into a 'pool' where market mechanisms would determine what price carriers would get for these slots - the suggestion being these would either go out to auction or prices would be fixed according to the nature of the airport (i.e. whether it is a hub or a spoke airport) and the time of the day (posted prices).

In proposal two, opening up airports to more competition, the EU proposes that carriers should have the right to buy and sell slots from other airlines should they wish to sell these (a practice known as secondary trading).

As with so many aspects of EU aviation policy such a scheme is fraught with problems and difficulties. Critics point out is it right to leave slot allocation to the dictates of the market? Indeed, who says this will produce a fairer allocation of resources? It also raises the interesting issue should parties other than carriers be allowed to trade in slots e.g. governments, airports, professional organisations, agents, etc? Should there even be caps on the number of slots held by individual carriers or alliances?

Some question whether a 10% re-allocation of Grand Father rights a fair figure? The UK government, for example, says it arbitrary and would not even support a 3% re-allocation. The also question who would post prices? And would prices be objective?

Elsewhere individual airlines, such as British Airways, has challenged whether the confiscating of Grand Father rights legal? They also question who would pay for this redistribution? In essence they see this as costly and political interference in their affairs. (TTG View From the Top 15.11.07)

Study Activity 15

Maybe we should be 'thinking outside of the box here'? Could capacity problems be reduced by getting people to switch to High Speed Rail services particularly on short-haul routes?

An alternative might be to get passengers to fly to secondary airports and transfer them to hubs by alternative transport modes. Here the Gatwick-Heathrow shuttle is illustrative. Indeed certain passengers might be only too willing to participate in such a scheme if they thought it would avoid the Heathrow T3 experience!

Another possibility could be to introduce a congestion charge at hub airports. This could be imposed on carriers while airlines using secondary airports would be exempt from such charges.

Yet another option might be more airport development.

The EU favours the former proposal using high speed rail). The AEA however says this would only account for 6-7% reduction of excess capacity and can only be viewed as a short term solution. Congestion charging is likely to prove universally unpopular with both passengers and the airlines. The possibility of building more airports would require a major change in public attitudes and better relations between airport developers and regional planners. As such, it is regarded as the least likely option.

- *Airport Charges*

EU proposals on airport charging are outlined in the document COM (2006) 820 final.

At present pricing for the use of airport infrastructure is determined at national level – by individual governments. Many airports in the EU are publicly owned and therefore it is in the interests of exchequers to maximise their return and prevent competition.

In the EU airport pricing is rarely transparent and information provided to carriers on any proposals to change these charges can be inadequate. This is an important consideration to airlines as these charges can account for between 4-8% of their operating costs (AEA 2007) In addition, the EU has argued that often carriers are not systematically consulted before any changes are made to airport charges

The EU's proposals for airport charging is based on *ICAO's (2004) Policies on Charging for Airports and Air Navigation Services, 7th Edition*

This argues for a number of basic principles:

- *Non-discrimination*: There should be no discrimination against any carrier. Costs should merely relate to the actual cost of facilities and the services provided

- *Transparency*: The airport operator should provide information to airlines on how airport costs are calculated. Carriers also have a responsibility to provide airports with their specific requirements e.g. traffic forecasts, fleet use etc

- *Quality*: The airport operator has a responsibility to provide the best possible service to carriers and their passengers

- *Differentiation of charges*: Charges will be set on the basis of fixed criteria. These will vary according to the level & quality of service

- *Security*: Funding for any improved security regulations should come outside of this pricing scheme

- *Regulation*: An authority will be established in each EU member state to ensure that these measures will be properly implemented.

Certain Problems are all to evident with the EU's proposal regarding airport charging. Because of quality differences, airport charges could vary quite considerably between airports (e.g. LHR compared to Southampton International) As such airport operators argue that charges are situation dependent and should not be determined by Brussels. It is also quite possible that there will be different charges between different terminals because of these quality differences (LHR T1-T5)

At present this policy does not have 'competence'. This means these principles are not legally binding. As such there is nothing stopping member states ignoring this directive.

The EU argues that this policy will give members a new framework and scope to change their airport pricing should they wish. However, why should they if the existing system is profitable? It will also take time money and political will to change the existing system. Currently there is no EU budget to implement these proposals.

Perhaps the only way to achieve a truly effective system is for these proposals to become law and to introduce a series of benchmarks linking charges to levels of service. Once airlines know exactly what airports will charge they would then use the most cost effective airports within the EU. This would then put pressure on other airports to raise their service levels and reduce their charges if they wanted to compete and win business.

Irrespective of the chosen solution, ultimately these proposals will not apply to 'small' airports (those of less than 1 million passenger movements p.a.)

CONCLUSION

This chapter has considered the thinking behind EU internal aviation policy. It has been shown that many individual policy initiatives are in their infancy. As a result rulings are often far from clear and subject to variable interpretations. The complexity of policy is only intensified by the need to produce a range of workable measures that extend across twenty six member states. Pressures from a number of powerful stakeholders both within and outside the aviation industry have also delayed proposals or have stopped them in their tracks. In essence EU internal aviation policy encapsulates the problems of developing and implementing mega-policy.

DISCUSSION QUESTIONS

1. Distinguish between 'internal' and 'external' aviation policy within the EU

2. Outline a number of ways in which the EU controls the aviation industry through setting the policy agenda.

3. Provide an example of where the EU has been at loggerheads with a NGO regarding its internal aviation policy.

4. Discuss why the EU might never effectively achieve a workable internal aviation policy.

5. Consider why environmentalism and concern for environmental issues might increasingly have to be taken seriously by airlines in the EU.

6. Why have efforts by the EU to introduce new proposals for slot allocation and modify airport charges caused considerable consternation in the aviation industry?

7. What justification is there for saving that the EU has no role to play in matters pertaining to civil aviation?

RECOMMENDED READING

Air Transport Portal of the European Commission (weekly)
www.ec.europa.eu/transport/air_portal

AEA Press Release (2005) EU External Aviation Policy: AEA Airlines Question Commission's Priorities @ www.luchtzak.be/article8034

Calleja, D (2004) EU/US Aviation Policy @ www.eurunion.org/news/speeches/2004

Council of the European Union (2007) Proposal for a Directive on Airport Charges. COM (2006) 820 final

Davidson, R (2006) Tourism in Europe, Pitman

Department for Transport (2003) National Air Traffic Services. Government Response to Select Committee Report @ www.dft.gov.uk/pgr/aviation

Department for Transport (2006) Reducing Air Traffic Delays. Government Response to Select Committee Report @ www.dft.gov.uk/pgr/aviation

Department for Transport (2006) UK Response to European Commission's Slot Allocation Consultation. @ www.dft.gov.uk/pgr/aviation

Department for Transport (2007) Aviation Safety. Government Response to Select Committee Report @ www.dft.gov.uk/pgr/aviation

European Commission DG for Energy and Transport (2005) Draft Commission Regulation Laying Down a Common Charging Scheme for Air Navigation Services, EC

Hamlin, G.W. (2006) Hold the Red Herrings, Let's Have Agreements on Direct Aid and Open Skies. Aviation Week and Space Technology, 165, 4, pg85

Page, S. J. (2005) Transport and Tourism: Global Perspectives, Second Edition, Prentice-Hall

IATA (2005) Air Transport Policy in the European Union: We Can do Better.

Salvarani, R (2006) EU Aviation Policy and Climate Change. DG Energy and Transport, European Commission

SERA (2006) EU Sustainable Aviation Policy: Lost in Translation?

Sparaco, P (2006) Low Cost Revolution. Aviation Week and Space Technology, 164, 13, pg50

Sparaco, P (2007) Italy's Error: Eurospective: Dinosaur Alitalia Needs to Get With the Plan. Aviation Week and Space Technology. 166, 7 pg44

Tyndall Centre for Climate Change (2006) Growth Scenarios for EU & UK Aviation. Friends of the Earth

US-Europe Aviation Security Poicy Summit (2007) Key Address @ www.eubusiness.com/transport/aviation-security

Wall, R (2006) Airport Agenda. Aviation Week and Space Technology. 164, 10 pg24

Wall, R (2006) Liability Language. Aviation Week and Space Technology. 164, 2 pg38

CHAPTER 13

EU External Aviation Policy

CHAPTER OULINE

Introduction

Competition

The Future of EU Aviation Policy

CHAPTER OBJECTIVES

Having read this chapter and undertaken the necessary study activities you should understand:

- What is meant by the term EU external aviation policy

- What EU external aviation policy hopes to achieve

- Some of the problems of implementing an external aviation mega-policy within the European Union

INTRODUCTION

In addition to proposing an internal aviation policy, the EU has also come up with a set of rules, regulations guidelines and directives governing its relationship with non-EU carriers and their governments.

To date, many of these policy directives have been levelled at trying to achieve a fair and equitable competition policy. Particularly targeted have been US carriers and the US Federal Government. In talks with their US counterparts, EU transport representatives have broached areas as diverse as guaranteeing take-off and landing spots for European carriers flying into the United States, EU ownership of US airlines and safety and security measures.

Discussions have been tense and stakes have been high. Indeed many would argue that this has been the most contentious aspect of EU aviation policy. It is to an analysis of these issues that attention is now turned.

COMPETITION

The EU proposes a number of bi-lateral agreements between itself and other countries/regions of the world. The idea is to cut 'red tape' (namely regulations) and allow more of a free market in aviation

The first flagship agreement has been between the EU and the US (The EU-US Open Aviation Area Agreement) first discussed in June 2003 and finally agreed in 2007. Others are proposed

The EU-US Open Aviation Agreement seeks to address a number of elements. These include:

1. *Regulatory co-operation & convergence*: working towards some basic fundamental rules and principles in the areas of security, safety, competition, state aid & environmental standards

2. *Market access*: where it is proposed EU and US Carriers should be allowed freedom to operate between any two points in their respective territories providing the carriers concerned do not compromise safety and security standards

3. *Ending restrictions on foreign ownership*: thereby making it possible for US airlines to own EU carriers and vice versa

4. *Removal of all restrictions on pricing* on all routes between the EU & the US

5. *Unlimited code sharing between EU & US airlines*

6. *Removal of all restrictions on EU cargo services to the US*

7. *The creation of new opportunities for EU airlines to wet lease air craft to US carriers for transatlantic flights*

8. *Giving European CRS providers the right to operate in the US*

At the same time the EU will seek to challenge a number of bi-lateral agreements in the European Court of Justice between individual EU member countries and third parties. Here the EU has consistently argued that these are illegal under the terms of the Treaty of Rome because they prevent other community carriers the right of establishment and operation laid down in the treaty

What might be the consequences of such actins? Here US consultants the Brattle Group suggest that an EU/US open aviation area would generate an extra 17 million passengers a year and would be worth $5 billion p.a. to the aviation industry. It would also create a considerable increase in jobs across both sides of the Atlantic

This said problems remain. Here the devil is in the detail. For example, what is meant by the term an open market? Added to this certain EU member airlines, such as British Airways, do not see the deal as reciprocal.

BA believes that the agreement allows US carriers' major access to European destinations but not vice versa. In particular they maintain that they will not be allowed to exercise traffic rights within the US.

Study Activity 1

On the basis of what evidence do they base this assumption?

The US Civil Reserve Air Fleet also believe that allowing foreign nationals to own US carriers is a threat to national security as they might not be prepared to carry US troops in times of national emergency.

Other concerns have also been voiced in the US. These centre on the possibility that higher paid US jobs will be substituted with lower paid EU workers (a view outlined in the House of Representatives on Capital Hill). In a similar vein US politicians have been concerned as to whether the agreement would just result in 'flags of convenience' airlines being established by EU operators in The States thereby under-cutting US operators. Continental Airlines have also raised the issue who would represent employees in merged airlines - US or European Unions?

Study Activity 2

Is there anything in any of these arguments or is it just a case of blatant protectionism on behalf of the American aviation industry?

A far as the EU goes American proposals to increase the amount of voting stock of potential European investors from 25-49% is seen as an irrelevance. This would neither give Europeans control of US carriers and it is felt goes against the principles of allowing a full merger or take-over.

Study Activity 3

Have any European carriers show an enthusiasm for taking over any of their US counterparts? If so, who?

The result is that the AEA Secretary General (2007) concluded this scheme 'is both over-ambitious and unfocused'

Similar efforts to negotiate such agreements with Russia and China have also come in for AEA criticism. Here the AEA see both as large markets 'but very much underdeveloped with specific infrastructural deficiencies'. In a stinging criticism of EU external policy in this area the AEA conclude:

'There should be demonstrable added value for The Community – this has not been proven. The countries concerned do not have mature economies nor do they pursue market orientated transport policies. Their airlines are known for abusive market practices. While these governments provide or are willing to provide excessive state aid to the aviation sector'

AEA (2007:23)

THE FUTURE OF EU AVIATION POLICY

How far the EU will be able to influence the future development of civil aviation will depend on the extent to which individual governments will give the Commission a mandate (or permission) to negotiate on their behalf.

Here it is necessary to get things into perspective. We have come a considerable way in developing an EU aviation policy. Just 15 years ago the industry was characterised by restrictive bi-lateral agreements, massive state intervention, fragmentation and national monopolies. Today the aviation industry operates in a completely different business environment. This is something for which the EU must be given some credit.

This said not everyone shares this view IATA for example believes all the EU has done is develop its own standards and impose them on its member's airlines(De Smet 2006). It has also criticised the actions of other bodies with years of experience of operating in this area. *(Could this possibly be IATA?).*

IATA maintain EU involvement in civil aviation has meant unnecessary complexity and cost and that it would be better suited to creating an environment that will allow the industry to grow. It sees no place for the EU in negotiating on issues such as ownership. Its actions have been political; it has distorted competition and has given subsidies to competitors (notably the railways).

IATA believes there are areas where the EU has no role to play e.g. war risk insurance and national security as these are government responsibilities and governments should pay for these things. The EU's efforts to pass these onto the airlines has merely resulted in crippling costs.

IATA argues allowing the privatisation of airports and air traffic control services has only turned public services into private and often unregulated monopolies. Here the only winner has been Treasuries. In short there needs to be a better balance between regulation and market forces.

The EU has been consistently guilty of ignoring the views of other stakeholders or not co-opting them into the policy making process. In a complex industry like civil aviation to ignore other views on technical issues, safety, service standards & international aviation law etc is a retrogressive step.

It concludes when making policy a thorough economic impact analysis of decisions should be made. All too often this has been insufficient or ignored by the EU. As a result its thesis is air transport policy in the European Union: we can do better.

CONCLUSION

In this chapter the key elements of EU external aviation policy have been discussed. It has been shown that this is an aspect of mega-policy that has many potential critics. Foremost amongst these have been national governments and industry regulatory bodies.

DISCUSSION QUESTIONS

1. Outline what you understand by EU external aviation policy.

2. What has been the cornerstone of this policy?

3. What criticisms have been directed against EU aviation policy and by whom?

4. What evidence is there to suggest that the efforts of the EU have been hindered by corporate and national protectionism?

CHAPTERS 11-13

A REVIEW

Chapters 11-13 have examined the concept of Mega-policy. They have concentrated on how EU aviation policy can be considered to be a good example of such a policy initiative.

Aspects of aviation policy have been considered. In doing so, the implications for the European airline industry have been discussed. The logistics and complexities of implementing mega-policy have also been broached. Here contrasting arguments have been offered as to the success (or otherwise) of these rules regulations guidelines and directives.

Before we move ahead to the final chapter it is important that you should be able to:

- Explain what is meant by the term mega-policy

- Outline how EU aviation policy might be considered to be a good example of such a type of policy

- Understand the difference between 'internal' and 'external' aviation policy

- Identify the components that constitute such policies

- Discuss the various merits of such initiatives

- Be conversant with a range of potential criticisms levelled against EU aviation policy and the role of the EU as a potential policy-maker.

- Reflect on whether EU aviation policy has made the European aviation industry more competitive.

A LOOK TO THE FUTURE

CHAPTER 14

Tourism Policy in the C21st

CHAPTER OUTLINE

Introduction

Tourism through the ages

The changing nature of tourism policy

New actors in a 'new' tourism policy arena

Should tourism policy making be left to the private sector?

From policy to strategy in a competitive paradigm

Conclusion

CHAPTER OBJECTIVES

Having read this chapter and undertaken the necessary study activities, you should understand:

- How the nature of tourism demand and the operational characteristics of the tourism industry has changed since the 1950s.

- How tourism policy has changed with structural and operational changes in the tourism industry.

- The increasing importance of the private sector in the process of making tourism policy.

- The arguments for and against partnerships and collective decision-making in policy-making.

- Whether tourism policy formulation and the execution of tourism policy can be left entirely to the private sector.

- The link between tourism policy and competitive strategy within a geo-political framework.

INTRODUCTION

The changing nature of the tourism industry, with its move away from mass tourism towards greater market segmentation, use of new technologies, differentiation of the product and adoption of new management styles demands a change in the substance of tourism policies. As we have seen in previous chapters, developments in the study of tourism policy have moved from pure promotion to product development to the current goal of maintaining competitiveness. In such an environment balanced partnerships between the public, private and voluntary sectors will be critical.

TOURISM THROUGH THE AGES

Tourism in the early post war years was characterised by standardised vacations to unseasoned tourists whose motives were very basic - the search for sun, sand and sea - at a modest price. The industry responded with rigid packages based on achieving significant economies of scale.

During the 1980s a great change occurred in the operational paradigm of tourism. This was a response to what Poon (1993) identified as new consumers; new technologies; new forms of production; new management styles and new prevailing circumstances. Tourism in the 1980s was characterised by the segmentation of demand, the need for flexibility of supply and distribution and achieving profitability through integration. New products were offered to the complex and diverse needs of the market.

Study Activity 1

In line with Poon's hypothesis, provide examples of the following developments in the tourism industry.

- *New methods of communication*

- *New methods of product distribution*

- *Flexibility in reservation, purchasing and payment systems*

- *New methods of product consumption*

- *Vertical and horizontal integration*

In the 1990s a new scenario for the tourism industry was to achieve competitiveness in which enterprises in the tourism sector must compete with enterprises from other sectors. In order for them to do so, this required:

- Improving tourism information systems e.g. demand requirements, strategy of the competition, making known the products on offer;

- Improving operational practices;

- Instilling a culture of quality and efficiency of service; and

- Adapting the product to the expectations of the client.

The C21st has seen an intensification of these trends.

THE CHANGING NATURE OF TOURISM POLICY

The contents of tourism policy have varied greatly over the years. First generation tourism policy was characterised by the objective, implicit or explicit, of stimulating mass tourism from a quantitative standpoint. Policy objectives typically included the maximisation of tourism revenues; improvement of income levels; the creation of employment and economic development.

Study Activity 2

Provide an example of such a policy.

The economic difficulties of the 1970s and the beginning of the 1980s, when the tourism industry was marked by successive phases of recession and growth, paved the way for a second generation of tourism policy frameworks.

Second generation policy frameworks have put the social, economic and environmental impacts of tourism to the fore (Krippendorf, 1982). Legal, economic and financial instruments are used in pursuit of the objective of increasing the contribution of tourism to the well-being of residents. Such policy initiatives have stressed product development (e.g. ecotourism, adventure tourism, urban tourism et al) and the need to make sectoral tourism policy congruent with general economic policies.

Study Activity 3

Once again, see if you can find an example of such a policy. Outline its aims and objectives and how the policy has been implemented.

The emergence of a new entrepreneurial paradigm in the mid 1980s changed the rules of the game for action in tourism policy. In this third generation of policy frameworks competitiveness has become the focal point of entrepreneurial tourism strategies.

Competitiveness, as we have seen in Chapter 3, can be defined as the capacity to generate profits in excess of the normal benefits in a sustainable way. It requires the implementation of methodologies geared to achieving quality in tourism services; organisational efficiency; administrative re-engineering and the evaluation of the social, economic and environmental repercussions of tourism on host regions.

Study Activity 4

Choose any <u>one</u> company or organisation and examine how it has targeted competitiveness as a policy objective.

NEW ACTORS IN A 'NEW' TOURISM POLICY ARENA

Earlier chapters examined who is traditionally responsible for formulating and executing tourism policy. Considerable attention was paid to identifying stakeholders and highlighting how these individuals input into the policy arena. What came through from this discussion was that policy making is not undertaken in a vacuum and that in the quest for competitiveness a partnership of the public, private and voluntary sectors is often required. (See the Banff-Bow Valley study - Chapter 10).

In policy making, the central role of the private sector is incontestable. It is difficult to envisage a competitive tourism industry in which the private sector does not play a key role. In many cases the private sector has acted as a catalyst for tourism development. In other instances it has brought new forms of management and production to the policy table. Concepts such as total quality management and process re-engineering originally developed in the private sector have found or are finding a place in the accommodation, catering, passenger transport and entertainment sectors of the tourism industry. Likewise the private sector has risen to the technological, marketing and financial challenges of joint ventures with the public sector.

Study Activity 5

Attempt to provide <u>three</u> examples of joint public-private sector partnerships in tourism, including at least one from the aviation industry.

SHOULD TOURISM POLICY MAKING BE LEFT TO THE PRIVATE SECTOR?

In the new entrepreneurial environment of the late 1990s and early C21st there seems no grounds on which to justify the inhibition of government action in the development of tourism or the privatisation of tourism administrations. This is despite efforts to the contrary (highlighted in Chapters 12 & 13) where increasing private sector involvement in civil aviation was reviewed. The quest for profitability is the driving force of modern tourism enterprises and securing citizen approval and the ensuing continuity of operations is what motivates tourism organisations.

The standard reasons for public intervention in the economy - to correct market imperfections and to provide public goods - are perfectly applicable to tourism activity in the C21st. Indeed it would be difficult to find sectors of this magnitude where the public sector does not play such an important role.

However, there is no doubt that certain areas that have traditionally come under the management of the public sector could be transferred to the private sector without too much difficulty. Mandatory tourism quality and classification systems could, for example, become voluntary and be put into the hands of the private or voluntary sector. The same premise could be applied to specific public tourism services, such as air traffic control services and the publication of guides and leaflets. Even in terms of tourism education and training, there appears to be no doubt that the private sector could share greater responsibilities.

It is, nevertheless, impossible to envisage a scenario in which all aspects of communication and promotion of destinations on national and world-wide markets, tourism area planning, the supply of macro infrastructure and services, design and supervision of multiple quality standards, protection of natural and cultural environments, and the co-ordination of tourism players - various levels of government departments, NGOs, enterprises, etc - could be tackled without government intervention, or solely with an intervention in terms of generic economic policy.

Finally, attention should be drawn to the important role of the so-called voluntary sector, made up of non-profit-making organisations, of people or private entities. NGOs have carried out important work in terms of tourism policy - and they still do - often in association with the private and public sectors. In this respect, there is a call to highlight their work in the field of information and promotion, the management of tourism development plans (environment and product), the provision of auxiliary services that improve the competitiveness of tourism regions (information, after-sales service, etc) and their collaboration with enterprises in terms of training, managing macro-products and others.

Study Activity 6

List the areas of policy making where you believe the functions of the public sector could be replaced by a private sector organisation. Give the reasons for your choice.

FROM POLICY TO STRATEGY IN A COMPETITIVE PARADIGM

The dramatic changes in direction that tourism policy has undergone has made it necessary for some countries to change their development strategies.

This strategy change has led to some traditional tourism sector policy objectives being given less importance (e.g. generating record visitor figures and tourism receipts) and to the targeting of specific new end objectives, such as making tourism enterprises and regions competitive and meeting social, economic and environmental objectives.

In this context, the success of tourism enterprises and destinations in the C21st not only hinges on the suitable exploitation of their comparative advantages, but also on the efforts made to ensure the creation of added value. Competitiveness will obviously depend not only on the functions pertaining to individual companies (research and development, training, management, production, marketing, after-sales services, etc) but also on the institutional and infrastructural framework of tourism activity.

Efforts that have been made to determine the instruments and means to make tourism competitive range from the translation of Porters principles to the development of specific models of tourism competitiveness (such as Ritchie and Crouch – discussed in Chapter 3).

Both analytical frameworks require congruent action by the private, public and voluntary sectors if favourable entrepreneurial conditions and competitiveness is to be achieved. The development of a coherent and workable EU aviation policy supports this theory. The operative schemes encompassed in this policy contain programmes and sub-programmes whose success has hinged on collaboration with players from the private and voluntary sectors. In this policy, the financial and entrepreneurial expertise of the private sector is important in terms of achieving competitiveness. At the risk of stating the obvious, mention should also be made of the need for co-ordination among the various levels of government of member states and between the various departments that constitute them.

CONCLUSION

The spectacular growth of tourism activity in recent decades has given rise to a qualitative transformation of the markets. Standardised tourism products geared to a homogenous demand - mass tourism - are being replaced by a new entrepreneurial paradigm which should respond to the super-segmentation of demand, the greater flexibility of supply, distribution and consumption, and the search for new sources of profitability in system economies and integrated values.

In this context, the focus of the objectives and instruments of tourism policy has been progressively shifting from the simple maximisation of visitors and tourism receipts to the creation of conditions for the competitiveness of tourism enterprises and regions, and from the primary use of promotional instruments to the application of specific models of tourism competitiveness that require the use of total quality management and process re-engineering methods.

An entrepreneurial utopian version of tourism policy, i.e. the quasi-privatisation of all tourism policy programmes, appears to be unsustainable. The existence of major external effects and other imperfections in tourism markets warrants public action. But this need is even greater in view of the complexity of the development and implementation of competitive strategies that affect both the internal aspects of the entrepreneurial environment and the macro tourism environment.

Nonetheless, the efficiency of public action in tourism is still at issue. A competitive public sector will require their powers and management processes to be redefined and increasing co-operation with the private and voluntary sectors. It is this that provides the challenge for policy-makers in the C21st.

DISCUSSION QUESTIONS

1. How have the operational characteristics of the tourism industry changed over the past forty years? Account for these changes.

2. How have policy frameworks changed to match new market paradigms?

3. What do you understand by the term competitiveness?

4. How has stakeholder involvement changed in the 'new climate' of policy formulation?

5. Why should the management of tourism services be left not to just the private sector?

6. How might a new entrepreneurial paradigm of tourism policy impact on the tourism management in a country?

RECOMMENDED READING

Poon, A (1993) Tourism: Technology and Competitive Strategies, CAB, Oxford.

Krippendorf, J (1982) Towards New Tourism. Tourism Management 3(3), pp. 135-148.

Osborne, D, Gaebler, T (2003) Re-inventing Government: How the Entrepreneurial Spirit is Transforming the Public Sector. Plume, New York.

Porter, M (1990) The Competitive Advantage of Nations, Macmillan.

Ritchie, B, Crouch, G (1993) Competitiveness in International Tourism: A Framework for Understanding and Analysis. WTO; Calgary.